Secret Keeper

Dr. Shree Walker

With
Michael D. Ison

Secret Keeper

Copyright © 2023 by Dr. Shree Walker (with Michael D. Ison)

All rights reserved. No portion of this book may be reproduced in any form without permission from the publisher, except as permitted by U.S. copyright law.

For permissions, contact shree.walker@resilientwalker.com.

This is a working memoir. In most instances, the information presented is largely subject to the author's memory and perspective. I have attempted to research verifiable facts; however, many instances will be delivered the way I remember them. Names have been changed in certain instances, but the truth, as I remember it, has remained the same and been borne out.

Unless otherwise noted, Scripture quotations are taken from the ESV® Bible (The Holy Bible, English Standard Version®). Copyright © 2001 by Crossway, a publishing ministry of Good News Publishers. Used by permission. All rights reserved.

ISBN: 9781088120071

Secret Keeper

Also by Dr. Shree Walker

Resilient Walker
Resilient Walker: Resiliency Guide
Trees, Dreams, Balloons & Things!
Educate Me!

To my true self, you are free!

Contents

Drama	1
One-Pager	8
November 1, 1986	10
Lies	16
More Lies	24
Chosen	29
Ring My Belle	36
Illicit Love	42
No More Lies	50
Truth	58
Every Scar	65
Nobody	72
Neverland	80
The List	89
Number Two	98
Mo Problems	105
Break	113
More Noise	124
Flannel Graph	139
Sheep, Wolf, Shepherd: Part 1	147
Sheep, Wolf, Shepherd: Part 2	153
Failure	162
Two Chairs	168
Two Scares	176
Two Scars	181
Presentation	190
Reflection	195
Trippin'	199
Peace	204
Create	211
Acknowledgments	217

Drama

I kicked my boyfriend's chest! I meant to. I meant to kick a hole right through him, kind of step through his body and leave him planted to the floor, impaled by my foot. I hoped he'd die—burn in hell for all I cared. Yeah. Burn in hell.

I cared. Clearly, I cared, or I wouldn't have kicked the hell out of him. I wanted him to burn in hell, to burn a fiery death that never extinguished, to writhe in pain for all eternity. He didn't. He flew back against the wall, and I started swinging.

I'd never been in a fight, but I swung like Mike Tyson. I fought that day. With lefts, rights, karate chops, fists of fury, I lurched at him.

He called out, "Shree! Shree! It's me!" I stopped, grabbed him, hugged him, and cried. At that moment, I didn't know who touched me, but I knew who I thought touched me: the monster with the friendly face and the secret fingers. The monster from my childhood whom I really wanted to send to hell.

Clearly, I have experienced some trauma. I've also created some drama. And I'm not talking about some baby mama drama that rap guys sing about. I mean real drama, like the kind of drama that ensues after kicking my boyfriend in the solar plexus and knocking the wind out of him. The kind of drama that races in the room and steals his breath away, making him fear me and making me fear myself. That kind of drama.

He won't touch me again. Not like that, he won't.

Here's what happened. He walked into the room, in the dark, and touched my shoulder. The audacity! Who did he think he was, my boyfriend?

The truth is he won't touch me again, not like that. Because he's afraid. Afraid to get kicked in the chest and punched in the face and cut to pieces if I get a hold of him. He's afraid of my trauma. I am too. That's why I kicked him, right in the chest.

Now he has trauma. Maybe he has his own PTSD (post-traumatic Shree disorder). I'm not making light of PTSD; I'm serious. He's afraid to touch me; I am afraid to be touched by him, and it all started with being touched.

Earlier in the day, I'd been scouring the internet, touching those keys, clicking those links, reaching out and touching my past. I had searched for the transcript from the court case of my abuser—the monster with the friendly face. He had touched me in secret, but the case blew wide open and now was public record. Now thirty-four years later, my past knocked on the door of my present, disrupting my future, as I reached back and touched it.

For some reason, on that day, I wanted to know. I wanted to remember what he said, what I said, what Momma said. What was said? What was said about the man who snuck into my bedroom at night, pulled me from the sheets, and dragged me into the bathroom? Probably nothing like: "This will still haunt her in the future when she kicks the hell out of her boyfriend as a grown woman" or "Even after she deals with the abuse, forgives the abuser, and teaches others about abuse, she'll still be abused."

I never found it. Not that night, anyway. I knew his name, date of birth, where he lived; I had even spoken to him a few years before he died. At my brother's funeral. He was my almost stepfather, after all. Former lover of my mother. Father of my brother. Father of my shame for so many years. He was the father of my secrets: my secrets started with him. And they never went away.

I don't blame him for everything. I blame him for what he did, but I don't blame him for all my other secrets. Just the first one. The big one.

Maybe it's better I never found the transcript and it remains a secret. If I read those words, heard those voices, let it all play in my head again, would it bring any solace? Or would it bring more trauma? And drama?

I suppose that's what this memoir is—an experiment of reaching back into my past, pulling those issues back to the surface, walking through them, and discovering if I heal.

Post-Traumatic Stress Disorder

When a war veteran survives the traumatic stress of battle and pushes himself past the limit of exhaustion, reaching the moment when he can rest easy, he can't. He dragged himself through the mire, got rescued by his platoon and collapsed after being transported to the hospital. Back then, he expended his energy on survival, and now he can't survive. He can't rest.

It haunts him. The memories do. The stress does. The gunshots ringing in his ears, the panic in his heart as the bombs exploded, the visions of holding his friend's head up as she drew her last breath. They haunt him. They live in his present mind, not in his past. He has a disorder. He's escaped, but he can't escape.

I know when I escaped my sexual predator, when I survived the monster and fell into the arms of an angel, I couldn't escape either. I couldn't rest. Just ask my boyfriend. (If he still is my boyfriend by the end of this book.) I spent a lifetime keeping secrets, hiding behind lies about myself, seeking the attention of men—other men, inappropriate men, untouchable men—trying to find rest. Trying to be special. So I could just breathe. But I couldn't. I couldn't rest.

Even after I forgave him for everything he did, what he took from me and what he gave to me, I didn't fully escape. I never fully escaped. No rest. No rest when my past snuck in and disrupted my present and my future. I wondered, *What if I touch it one more time? Will I make peace with my past, move beyond it, and seek out a new life where I am wholly healed?*

As I write this, I have my doubts. Don't get me wrong. I believe in the possibilities. I'm not a Debbie Downer, a Negative Nancy, or a Pessimist Pam—I'm a Resilient Walker, and I know my name. I have doubts because I am not sure touching all my secrets again will bring the healing I want. Maybe I'm broken and need to accept it.

Back to the war veteran and the PTSD. The man I'm visualizing lost a leg right below the knee. He's dangerously good looking, with broad shoulders and a cast-iron jaw. A total overcomer. After the amputation and receiving a prosthetic leg, he trained his body and mind to absorb the punishment of running. Not just running in general but running marathons. Ultramarathons. Today, when he's not training, he's speaking. He's encouraging other veterans and amputees to overcome. Large crowds gather to see this brave hero speak into broken lives.

At night, he takes off his leg to go to sleep. The phantom pains start. His foot itches. The one that's not there, which he hasn't seen in years. With nothing to scratch, he only has a reason to scratch, a phantom itch that makes him feel insane. Since he can't scratch what's not there. He rolls over, kisses his lucky wife good night, and falls into a deep sleep.

Since he's an overcomer, he doesn't have nightmares: he sleeps the slumber of a man at peace with himself, in harmony with the universe. He probably even has chiseled abs, and his bride's a supermodel. But he can't scratch what's not there. He's missing a piece of himself. He's an amputee.

That's why I have my doubts. He's still injured. He's not any less of a man for missing a piece of his leg; rather, he's more of a man. And I love him. I want to be him—well, if I were a man. Maybe I just want to be with him. Which means I still have issues from my past. But he's still an amputee.

And I'm still abused.

Post-Traumatic Shree Disorder

I've been living with myself for a long time, forty-four years. Neither my abuse nor my abuser defines me. They are part of me, but they don't define me. Just like the war veteran who lost his leg, I can't escape my past; it's part of me. I'm not trying to escape it; I'm trying to heal from it. Is this it? Is this what healing looks like? Kicking people in the chest and throwing bows like Anderson Silva?

I don't think so. I don't believe so. I believe I can walk away from my past and push into the future and swim in the ocean of grace. Maybe instead of a Resilient Walker, I'll be a resilient mermaid, flipping my tail against the current and loving every minute of it. But I still have my doubts.

I've been taught the best way to heal from the past is to deal with the past. I suppose all victims of PTSD must step back into their past and look that issue right in the eye and fight it, forgive it, or walk away from it. Or stay stuck. I had dealt with my past before, so why did I go searching late at night to find a transcript of a thirty-year-old case and drop-kick my boyfriend? I don't know.

Can I recover from being me? Can I recover from being Shree? Will I carry this post-traumatic Shree disorder around with me forever? Yet deep down, I believe I can learn to accept myself for who I am, for what I've done—all the bad and all the good—and come out whole.

Because just like I know there are monsters with friendly faces and angels with scars, I know I can be a little bit of both. I don't judge. I don't even judge myself. Besides, I'd make a terrible judge: to me, everybody's guilty and everybody's innocent. Instead, I will try to accept what I discover on this path I walk into my past and connect to my present. And if I discover that walking back through my past wasted my time, then I hope to accept that I learned a lesson from that too.

My post-traumatic Shree disorder will transform into a pretty tremendous Shree discovery. I'll be whole if I accept that *whole* sometimes means broken and put back together. I hope my boyfriend will be whole too—when he can breathe again.

Poetic Justice

I love poetry. I love Atticus's poetry best. Poetry touches me in places where I need to be touched. Unlike those secret touches from the past. The right poetry reaches inside me and pulls; it evokes compassion that lies dormant for far too long. In my mind, the veteran who runs the ultramarathons serves poetic justice to the world. He becomes known for what should have kept him unknown. He's not known for his missing leg; he's known because he runs without one.

I have a poem I borrowed from a friend that I've rewritten. I've made some changes, with his permission, to fit me. Here goes:

Shree Walker

"Secret Keeper"

I walk this path of Discovery,
Maybe I'll discover me,
And find inside the ability
To accept and then to see.

These secrets though dark and damp,
Need some light from my lamp.
I'll shine upon it and revamp,
My perspective on the stamp.

The stamp you see on my head,
What I should've done, should've said,
Not a victim, better off instead,
I'll change the message, what is read.

And find inside that I'm not mine,
Knowing my life was not kind,
I'm not dumb; I can read the sign:
Not my own; I need the Vine.

The Vine you see, to be fully me,
I'll confront these secrets I can't be,
And realize what I'm blind to see,
That freedom lives inside me.

At the end of my seminars, I have the audience complete a series of statements and answer a few questions. At the end of each chapter, I've left you one statement to complete or one question to answer. Please complete the following statement:

Secret Keeper

Understand

My experience reading this chapter was

One-Pager

Nobody reads the preface. This is my second memoir. I hate when authors constantly refer to previous works, so I mitigated that with this one-pager. In *Resilient Walker*, I wrote about what happened to me, what I experienced, what I overcame. I told on *them* and revealed myself.

In this memoir, I tell on myself, digging through my past, looking at me. It ain't pretty. I ain't tryin' to be. So, this is a cautionary tale. If you read and think, *That's so bad!* Yes, it is. I'm not advocating. I'm confessing. Sure, others get hit by the bus in the process, but I'm telling on myself. And in telling, I risk revealing I don't know when to keep my mouth shut.

Yes, some explicit language and content are present. No, I don't provide details. It's not *that* kind of book.

In the end, I believe we carry ourselves with us—the good and the bad—and hopefully, we learn from both. Then release the past and keep moving forward. Walk on, little one. Walk on!

Analyze

After reading this chapter, I feel

Shree Walker

November 1, 1986

The blue ink tear-stained the white page. Momma scrunched her face as the tears fell, forming a puddle on the ink expressed from her pen. She filled in the blanks of the black-and-white page, and the blue ink merged with tears, staining the page a darker blue than the sky but lighter than the weight in her heart. Her heavy hand pressed the weight of abuse on the page, my abuse, and the name of my abuser: her former husband, the monster with the friendly face.

I always admired my mother's handwriting, bold yet artistic; when she wrote, she rolled her personality onto the page. Momma loved expressing herself in dramatic ways: yelling at the refs during basketball games, styling hair in the kitchen, decorating the house with inflatable palm trees, and giving advice. On November 1, 1986, she gave no advice. Only her blue truth, her black-and-blue truth. She held the pen in one hand, a court document in the other, and the grief in her heart, which expressed itself in inky tears. I crowded against her. "What's wrong, Momma?"

"Nothing, baby. It's just this damn pen." The pen worked fine, but the tears muddled her message and disrupted the flow of her personality. The ink communicated that my abuser had touched me, and she didn't do anything about it. She didn't do anything because she didn't know.

For whom did the ink run: for me, for Momma, or for all the lost hopes and dreams bleeding into nightmares? I didn't know. I'll never know. I stood by Momma's side, captured in the moment of tear-stained ink.

Mumford and Sons sing the song "White Blank Page," and they sing of a white blank page and a swelling rage. Momma's spilled over the brink, off the edge, and onto the table. She didn't want to talk about it. She didn't want to write about it. She didn't want to think about my tear-stained skirt.

Court

I don't remember what day of the week we went to court, but I remember the date on the document read November 1, 1986. As a nine-year-old, the significance of the day eluded me. That morning, I merely did as I was told. I got dressed and put on a white shirt and a matching skirt. Blue leaves blew on my skirt, matching the stained-ink paper Momma carried in her clenched hand. In my clenched hand, I held onto a Mickey Mouse purse. The cross-body strap held the purse against me, but I used my hand for safekeeping.

We walked inside the courthouse; its long halls and storied ceilings frightened me. I looked through the transparent top of my plastic purse for the objects of security. Inside it, I kept colored pencils: a way of escape. (Today, I still keep colored pencils and pull them out when my emotions push past the red line. Or when I feel blue.)

Looking into the courtroom, I felt insignificant. Walking in, the overgrown room buzzed with brown and gray suits, ordered talk, and grave faces. The faces run blank in my mind, blurred white and red, black and brown. The only face I remember vividly is that of Mickey, gazing up at me, asking me to open the purse and color. The transparent top of the Mickey Mouse purse had no color. His thoughts were exposed in reds, blues, greens, and yellows. I could see his story. Someone else would hear mine in five, four, three, two, one . . .

I spoke. What I said, I don't remember. Momma spoke. What she said, I don't remember. The lawyers and the judge spoke, what they said . . .

All I remember is that stupid date: November 1, 1986. And my skirt, the tear-stained sheet, and Mickey. One more thing I remember is I didn't

Shree Walker

color. The page remained white and blank. Since I can't remember, I'm only left with what I know. One thing I can't forget is he didn't go to jail. Not on November 1, 1986.

Dates

I love dates. I've had several. My fondest date with my dad was the day he picked me up on his motorcycle and we rode to the park and colored. I used crayons on that date. He smelled wonderful, like a man. I acted like a princess, like a little girl.

Dates are important. I remember dates, like the day Malcolm X died, February 21, 1965. One of my favorite autobiographies, *The Autobiography of Malcolm X*, showed me that a person can fill their life with passion in one direction, undergo a metamorphosis, and passionately pursue another direction. A contrary direction. A direction with more purpose and more salvation. When I closed the book, the date of his death etched itself into my memory.[1] Momma remembers dates too. My old boyfriend from high school, No Name, does too. We're date people.

When I searched through my past, digging for the transcript of that court case, trying to discover what happened, I didn't know the significance of the date when the monster with the friendly face came into the world.

Having worked in Metro Public Schools in Nashville for years, I investigated court transcripts several times. Working with special populations (students with special circumstances), I sleuthed my way through websites and documents to understand those circumstances fully. When I attempted to research my assailant, I thought it would be easy. It was easy—like cutting off my nose to spite my face.

I opened the website, inserted the necessary information, and discovered that due to the commonality of my almost-stepfather's name, I needed his birth date—who knew Monster with a Friendly Face was such a common name? No problem. I asked Momma. She didn't know. I asked for my brother's birth certificate; she said it burned in a fire. I asked for their marriage certificate—never existed. I asked for a hammer; she gave me a

---

[1] The chapters on his death were included posthumously.

banana. She and my "stepfather" never married. He fathered a son with her, molested me, and stepped.

I let it go and moved on—content to leave the past in the past. Years passed, and I forgot the whole sequence of events, but I didn't forget the sequins. One night, while preparing for a masquerade ball, I donned a sequin gown and fixed my face in the mirror. That moment revealed a perfect analogy for how I felt at the time: masquerading in a beautiful gown and having a ball. But what lay beneath? I looked into the mirror to ask what it saw, but Momma made me laugh as she slinked into the room like a gliding ballroom dancer.

I said, "What you want, Momma?" She didn't make a peep. I asked her again.

All she said was, "Look."

She held a picture of a tombstone, my brother's tombstone. *How eerie.* The closer I looked, the more the dates confused me. They got the dates wrong. He wasn't born before me. What was Momma trying to tell me? I looked back at the name and discovered it wasn't my brother's tombstone. It belonged to his father—my monster. He and my brother share similar names. Momma handed me what I needed: a picture of the past.

February 21, 1965, was the day Malcolm X died and the date *he* arrived. Ironically, the perpetrator of my hope died the day the perpetrator of my death was born. Of all the possible ways I could have reacted at the moment, I chose to share an odd truth that trembled on the precipice of my lips. No tears rushed from my eyes, and no gush of laughter escaped my mouth. I didn't inhale a shocked gasp. I let the words jump off the edge of my lips to an untimely death. "It's done."

That's it. It's done. He's dead. I knew when he arrived and when he left. The past was the past, and I left the past in the past, buried beneath the grass and tombstone. Buried in the grave.

Lies

That's a damned lie. I didn't leave no past in the past. I waited until a more opportune time, late at night, with nobody around, searched that junk up, never found it, and kicked my boyfriend right in the chest. I couldn't leave well enough alone. My almost- stepfather lay cold and stiff under the ground, buried in the past. I forgave him, wrote about him in my first memoir, and moved on. I thought I was healed, but I had lied to myself. A damned lie.

Yes, I know I *should* write a *damn* lie, but this lie damned me. My dammed-up emotions released like a torrent of profane spit upon my present. And my lie damned me to circling back around to face it once again. Should I face my past? Maybe I should have torn out that white blank page, drawn a tombstone, and written, "Gone but not forgotten" in blue, tear-stained ink.

Secret Keeper

Evaluate

Before reading this chapter, I thought

After reading this chapter, I now think

Shree Walker

Lies

"Secrets make you special." I once had a secret that made me special. Here's my story of a scandalous secret that made me special. I love telling the same story two and three times. A story can replay itself in my mind two hundred times or two hundred million times. Each time more twisted. A story can replay itself in my life two hundred or two hundred million times. Each time more twisted. I'll tell the story again. It'll be our secret.

"Secrets make you special," he whispered, pulling me down the hall, headed for the bathroom. He smelled like lotion and sweat washed in a vile of aftershave. I wondered if Momma heard us. Did she hear the creaking door close or his pants dropping to the floor? Did she hear my silent tears, my cries of distress? Of course not. They emitted no sound. Only tears.

He pulled me to the floor, on my knees, in front of him. He told me to do things that made him feel special, that made me a secret. "Secrets make you special," he whispered again.

I didn't want to do those things. But I wanted to be special, and I loved being a secret. I secretly wondered if he loved me more than Momma. If I were more special. But I didn't want to do those things. I wanted out. Away. I wanted to sleep through the night holding a teddy bear like a normal girl. Or ride on the back of a horse while holding onto a handsome prince like in a fairy tale. But I was in the bathroom. On my knees.

I made up my own story to escape. I escaped in my mind to a story where a man loved me more than any other. I performed in my story as an actress on the stage. In my story, the actress acted for an audience of one because the secret made it special.

Sometimes I wonder why he didn't go jerk off. Why ruin my life in addition to his? I must have been special. The secret proved I was special. People who trust each other have secrets between them—things only the two of them know. That's what makes their relationship special. I must have been special, or he would have gone to the bathroom alone.

I crawled out of that bathroom multiple times and learned I was special. Men wanted me. And not just any men—taken men. The bigger the risk, the more special I was. The larger the secret, the more tantalizing I must be. Victoria's Secret had nothing on me. Her man left her for me, for my secret. I had to keep it. If I lost it, I'd no longer be special. I'd be broken.

Secrets Made Me Special

Daddy taught me that. I know I wrote my secrets started with my almost-stepfather, and they did. *My* secrets did. But Daddy's secrets began with me, or at least the secrets I knew about.

Daddy and Momma had three children together by the time they were nineteen and unmarried. I came first. Daddy grew up on the right side of the tracks. Momma grew up on the left, the left behind side.

Daddy's wealthy family lived in a big house with large rooms and trophies on the wall. Momma's house "didn't have no trophies," so Daddy and Momma made a trophy together. And they named her Shree Denise Walker. Then Daddy did what people do with all trophies—hide them in the back room, way in the back, in the closet, where they can't get stolen.

That's what Daddy did. He hid me, so I wouldn't get stolen, so I wouldn't lose my *special*. When he had another baby, he kept it a secret. When he met another woman, he kept me a secret. Because he loved me. We loved each other, and he didn't want me to be harmed, so he buried me like a precious diamond. When I met the other women or their families,

I pretended to be a lump of coal. They shouldn't see the diamond, or something bad might happen.

When Daddy came by and picked me up, we went places in secret. Together. We didn't bring my little brother or sister. We needed the time together—alone, exclusive—because I was so special. The park. The mall. The store. Wherever we went, I told nobody I was his princess. Princesses get kidnapped.

Being the Girl on the Side Made Me Special

My high school boyfriend made me a secret too, so I never kicked his chest. I rubbed it. He was broad and strong, and college scouts recruited him more than any other player in our area. Talk about special. He snuck over at two in the morning, and we sat on the front porch and stared at the stars. He snuck over in the evenings, and we studied by candlelight. He snuck into the bedroom, and we made each other feel special.

We even had secret names for each other. He called me Re, and I called him . . . No Name. He moved away for college, and I followed, but I stayed a secret. He had a child. I knew he'd made me his girlfriend, so why did he have a child with another woman? Then he had another. I realized I was the girl on the side. And that made me incredibly special. The most special. I must be better than her because he'd leave her to come see me.

He had another child. Three children and none with me, but we didn't need children because he wanted me all to himself. The girl on the side only masquerades as "on the side" because she's so valuable. He risked his relationships, his reputation, and his respect all for me. I hid in the shadows because hiding made me valuable. The small diamond we promenade on our finger, but the big diamond we keep in the safe. I was the big diamond.

I had no name in his book, but I bet I had a name in hers. What was her name again? Mrs. No Name? Not special. Not in my book, anyway. She never made it into our secret club. No Name. No Face. No Password. She got the name, but I knew all his secrets. I was good for the side, good for the ride, and good for the hide.

We protected each other. That's what people who love each other do. Protect. We protected each other. We shared our secrets, kept the secrets, and were each other's secrets. Victoria would be proud. Camilla too.

Being the "Other" Woman Made Me Special

In fairy tales, the handsome prince crosses over an alligator-infested moat, tunnels through a series of booby traps, slays the dragon, and rescues the princess. They ride off on his faithful steed and live happily ever after in each other's arms. In real life, the handsome prince dashes out of the house to get away from the evil witch, crosses over an alligator-infested moat, tunnels through a series of booby traps, and slays the princess. Again and again.

But then he puts her back. Back behind the alligator-infested moat, back behind the booby traps, back in the castle to wait for the next time he can reach her. He must return to fight the evil witch, to conquer the world, so he can protect his true prize. He keeps her hidden away, away from the pain, danger, and risk. Away from the world. Where she is supposed to be. In the castle, like a queen.

As Queen Shree, I ruled my castle well. My Prince Charming ran to me often, dodging the clutches of the evil shrew. He risked it all. His name was Leon.

Leon made miracles happen. He bought and sold and repaired broken things, made millions, and held an office. He was married and his children attended private school. Speaking to groups, he infused his listeners with energy, speaking of "family values" and "equity." All the while, he stole out of the house to get to me. How he pulled it off, I don't know. He worked miracles, and nobody could catch him.

I met Leon at a mechanic's shop. My jeep needed some work; his Mercedes did too. He plunged into flirtatious behavior, drawing me in like the only girl in the world. Touching my arm as he spoke, captivating me with those eyes, imbibing me with that British accent, I knew I was a prize. My senses tingled, telling me something like a mirage stood between me and that man, so I asked, "You got a girlfriend?"

"Yeah."

He continued pursuing, perusing the goods, seeking my affection.

"You live with her?"

"Yeah, but what's that got to do with talking to you? What's that got to do with getting a date with you?"

He chose me! My pride ricocheted off the sky and never came down to earth. If he had her but chose me, then I must be better—worthy of being pursued. I tried to talk myself out of it. *Girl, what are you doing? He's got a girl. You don't need to be messing with no man who's already got a girl. But if he's got a girl and he's willing to cheat with me, then she must not be that special. Not like I am.*

We went to dinner, had sex, built a relationship. He had two phones; I had both phone numbers. He had two lives; I held both ends. If I told, I could ruin him. If I kept the secret, I kept him. He came over on Monday, Tuesday, Wednesday, Thursday, Saturday, and Sunday—after church. We had long conversations about life, relationships, our careers, and our dreams.

I can't cook that well, but I can cook well enough to make a man stay. We never watched movies or television. We talked. He was interested. I was interesting. One day I asked, "If you got a girlfriend, why do you come see me?"

"She's boring."

I decided I would never be boring. In fact, I became the crazy camping lady. I purchased a popup tent and pitched it right in my living room. He never knew what to expect! I kept it interesting, kept it moving. Our love blossomed.

I loved being the "other woman." He chose me. He risked everything for me. He pursued me. The evil witch could never be as good as me because he never stopped pursuing me. I must be chosen.

"Mirror, Mirror, on the wall, who's the fairest of them all?"

"Not you, you're not the one, she's the secret, the chosen one!"

"Mirror, Mirror, on the wall, who's the fairest of them all?"

"You can't, but she can, if Shree can't keep him, no one can!"

The evil witch's mirror told her the truth. She couldn't see me, but I was number one, and she was number two. Leon and I went on and on like this for months, until her mirror cracked. One day, I sent a text. He texted back. I sent another. He texted back, but differently like he didn't know whom he was talking to. I stopped. She started.

Secret Keeper

The evil witch raised her head and cast an evil spell. She spat vitriol and violence my way. Good thing for the mirror because her words bounced off and hit her in the face. The mirror reflected. Unlike a window, she couldn't see through it. All she got back was her ugly face.

I blocked him. Ended it. He slipped up. He didn't protect his princess and let her be exposed to the witch. I returned to being the queen.

Being a Secret Made Me Smart

I'm not stupid. I loved the chase, but I didn't want to be chased. Let him clean up his mess. I blocked him and stayed cool in the knowledge that as the interesting, chosen, secret one, I'd never be boring. I'd never get caught. I made miracles happen too. My castle would never be ransacked because I was the queen. Not some stupid princess waiting to be rescued. The knight got himself killed by the evil witch, and it was time to move on. Bury the past and embrace the present.

That's the electrifying thing about being a secret: I got what I wanted, and then I got gone! The rules didn't apply to me because I made my own rules and slid by in the night without any personal casualty. Those who got caught weren't good secret keepers. They didn't understand the game as I did. They got played.

That would never happen to me. I played to win every game, and keeping secrets was part of my strategy. There are two golden rules of secret keeping. One kept me smart, and the other kept me safe. The first is "Don't get caught." The second is "If you do get caught, make someone else pay the price." I'd let Leon pay his own bail while I bailed. I moved on, leaving the past in the past.

Like I do.

Being a Secret Made Me Stupid

I looked in my own mirror and asked, "Mirror, Mirror, what do you see?" But I couldn't see. The mirror fogged over. I wiped it off, scrubbed and polished it, and wiped away the debris. But I couldn't see. The room filled with smoke. I choked. My mirror wasn't cracked or shattered or broken. What was wrong? I looked again. What fogged up the mirror?

I did. My breath did. I fogged my own mirror with my rancid, stanky breath. I looked again and said, "Mirror, Mirror, what do you see?"

"I see the dragon looking back at me."

The dragon, the beast of burden, peered back with red, beady eyes, a forked tongue, and fiery breath.

I asked again, "Mirror, Mirror, what do you see?"

"I see a lying, cheating, viscous Shree."

Then my mirror broke. My self-image revealed itself as a perfect lie. My conscience and the reality of who I once was and who I had become would not allow my secrets to secret themselves in the past. I must face them. I decided to change. I would not be "the other woman" any longer. I'd be me, the only me I knew how to be. The secret had made me stupid, not special. That was a lie. I knew the truth, and the truth would set me free. Being a secret didn't make me special—but being noticed did.

Secret Keeper

Create

After reading this chapter, I will restore myself by

Shree Walker

More Lies

Being noticed made me special! During high school, everybody knew me. Although I moved multiple times and attended four different high schools, everyone knew me. They knew me from the drama club, the creative writing club, and the journalism club, as an athletic trainer, track star, cadet battalion leader, performer, speaker, and all-around cool girl. I got noticed.

Although I came from the ghetto, people didn't know me as ghetto. I never wore the bamboo earrings and long, fake, neon nails. I still admired them—and *eww!*—I wanted them so bad at times, but I didn't want to be the stereotypical Black girl. I never wore them. I was not ghetto.

People didn't know my past or my secrets; they only noticed the Shree I wanted them to see, and I liked it that way. Even though getting noticed made me special, I had my standards—at least, I thought I did. I hid my secrets so they wouldn't get noticed, and I shone like a star in *respectable* areas.

Later, as a teacher, everybody noticed me. I won Teacher of the Year, Most Influential Educator, and a slew of other awards. Being one of the few Black teachers at Hillsboro High School got me noticed. Don't get me wrong: when I taught at the alternative school or Jere Baxter, which were both predominately Black schools, I got noticed too. Because I was good.

Good with students of diverse populations, good with parents, good at solving problems, good at getting noticed. The more people noticed me, the more I got promoted, and promoted, and promoted.

When I joined the navy, everybody noticed me. During basic training, I got promoted to chief yeoman. In boot camp! I had all these eighteen- and nineteen-year-old kids reporting to me, looking to me to lead the way. They all knew my name.

When I returned to school to pursue my master's degree, the professors called on me in class all the time! "Ms. Walker, what do you believe is the best way to differentiate lessons when you have mixed ability groups?" I'd answer, and they'd stare at me like I was a billionaire. Noticeably articulate. Noticeably profound. Noticeably different. The other students learned my name and wanted to team up with me. They wanted to get noticed too.

I eventually pursued an administrative position as a principal, then a dean, and I managed multiple sites, multiple schools, multiple students, and multiple teachers. As a result, I received multiple accolades. And I got promoted. I took the position as a 504 coordinator, then supervisor, then the director of special populations for Metro Nashville Public Schools, and then all the teachers and principals had to know my name.

I earned my doctorate from David Lipscomb University. Me, a little Black girl from Los Angeles, Watts even, and I got noticed. Doctors get noticed, right? Dr. Shree Walker.

I volunteered for speaking engagements, where I spoke about abuse and the effects of abuse. I spoke about recovering from abuse and trauma. My speaking disrupted people's thinking. When audiences heard about my trauma from being molested, raped, and abandoned, they noticed.

I got paid to accept speaking engagements. I no longer volunteered; I got invited. Requested. Begged. Surely, the world noticed. I spoke to superintendents, judges, politicians, entertainers, athletes, the whole gamut. Notice anything yet?

Being noticed made me special. I wrote a book. Then another. And another. And another. Four books in five years, while leaving the education industry and tackling an entrepreneurial venture. In a few short months, I garnered great attention and successfully launched a public speaking career. I started a movement called *Die Empty*, and it moved people to join. Everyone noticed.

So why the hell didn't I notice?

Someone Special Noticed

I learned long ago that achievements never made me special. I left the navy, worked at Hillsboro High, and had a crisis of existence. Some call it an existential crisis. I called it a total breakdown. When I melted down and surrendered my life to Christ, I learned that the achievements satiated an ever-growing appetite in me. Until I got hungry again. Probably the next day.

Along the way, I met David. Done with the lies of the past, the Leons, and the No Names, I settled into a loving, long-term, monogamous relationship. We met. We marveled. We married. He noticed me and I noticed him, and I knew I was special.

The thing about meeting someone special was that sometimes it deprived me of what made me special. I had to share. Living with a special person created another problem. Special people noticed me, all of me, the beautiful and the ugly. The scars. David noticed and still accepted me for my scars—he was an angel with scars too.

He noticed something else too: only being noticed made me *feel* special. Being special—being special to him—amounted to very little. Not enough. Not enough to keep the glass full and the love pouring over. It poured out.

No longer getting noticed by my man and only being accepted by my man poked a hole in my cup. I became a funnel. Love poured in. Love poured out. Right on the floor, begging someone to notice. Love poured in; love poured out.

Sure, other men noticed me, but David and I committed our lives to each other. Who cared if they noticed? I loved David for good. Forever. He accepted me in spite of my unrelenting desire to get noticed. Love poured in; love poured out.

But I got out. David and I divorced. I'll save that story for last. I'm not ready to tell it yet. I wonder if resurrecting that story will bring me healing. At least it will get me noticed.

Secret Keeper

The First Four Years

Laura Ingalls Wilder, the famed author of *Little House on the Prairie*, wrote several memoirs of her childhood and teen years. She also wrote a memoir about her first four years of marriage, aptly titled *The First Four Years*. For years, I hated that book. She detailed the struggles she and her husband, Almanzo, suffered. Some at the hands of Mother Nature, some at the hands of sickness, some by each other's hands. She chronicled the loss of a child and pain, severe pain. The book depressed me. Surely, marriage couldn't be that difficult. She was right.

Much like Wilder, I needed to write. I needed to right some wrongs of my past, and I needed to write about the last four years. Yet being drawn back into my past sucked me into the ever-present tug to determine what made me who I am. I knew I needed to write about the first four years. The years that led to the last four years.

Middle school, where it started. I must write about my middle school years that defined my fears and formed my feelings. The years that told me who I was and where I belonged. The years when looking in the mirror brought me shame, when dancing privately felt like freedom and dancing publicly felt like a cage. The years when walking into a bathroom filled with girls brought a shudder, getting noticed felt like stabs in a voodoo doll, and church brought my only solace.

It's another world, middle school, and it left some scars. David touched some of those scars. They weren't healed. They scarred him too. But middle school also meant fun, excitement, and trying new things. I'm a lot of things, but one thing I'm not is afraid to try new things. Middle school meant fun and pain, all wrapped up in a bow.

And lies. In middle school, I learned to lie. Not to keep secrets but to tell lies.

"Mirror, Mirror, on the wall, what's the biggest lie of them all?"

Shree Walker

Apply

Because of my experience reading this chapter, now I will

Chosen

We spoke without words. He peered across the room into my eyes, into my soul. A quick glance, a soul flutter, the bat of my eyes, and his longing gaze created a desire in me. A desire to be chosen, held tight, embraced like I mattered more at the moment than the moment itself, erupted.

He stood, long and lanky, by the punch bowl. With his arrogant chin pointed toward her. His girlfriend, Wanette, laughed at him coyly, brushing his arm with her hand, as if to say, "Oh, shut up. Just shut up." I wanted her to shut up.

The lights from the ceiling shone on him, illuminating his form—powerful—by the table, by the punch bowl—in my mind. Lafayette. Lafayette of the caramel-colored skin, the light brown eyes with no clouds, the perfect smile, the infectious laugh, the longing look. Lafayette, the boyfriend in my mind. If only he knew he was mine.

My sweaty palms clammed up into starfish. My hands hung like weights at my sides. He had a girlfriend. I couldn't approach him. But the way he looked at me! The way his smile called me over, asked to take me in his arms, and dance until the lunch bell rang. The way he moved told me, told me, told me that he wanted—then he grabbed her hand.

Shree Walker

Lafayette grabbed Wanette by the hand and led her to the dance floor. He graced the floor with his six-foot frame, standing tall above the other boys. He pushed her away, and she held his hand with hers. He pulled her close, and she fell into his body, his chest: crème—not cream because *Lafayette* is French after all—and mocha, they danced. From above, he looked into her eyes, taunting her, calling her name, spelling out that he chose her. He pulled her closer. I could see her body radiate with desire. She looked up; he looked down, and they leaned toward each other.

The lunch bell rang. Disrupting the romance in my mind, the lunch bell rang and ended the middle school dance, but it began a new pursuit for me. I wanted to be . . . chosen.

I Loved the Boys

From a young age, I loved the boys. I mean, like elementary school young. Where I grew up, kids played "hide and go get it," but I didn't play those kinds of games because the abuse taught me better. I didn't like small spaces with men I couldn't control. No, I didn't play hide and go get it, but I loved the boys.

I loved me some brown boys too. In middle school, I loved the Latino boys equally: José, Jorge, Marcos, Raúl, Michael, on and on. They all got much love from me. Not much touch, much love. I loved them, but they didn't love me back. Well, I take that back. I guess they got a little touch from me, but not much. I used to let Michael rub my booty. Nothing ever happened, but I'd let him rub my booty. We were friends; he didn't like me like that, so I guess we were booty-rubbing friends.

Friend Zone

In middle school, I joined the cadets. Left, right, left, remember? I walked straight and tall with perfect form. That's all I could do. I had no form, no shape, just straight, skinny, and tall. Not a big seller in the Black and brown neighborhoods. Through the cadets, I met José and Raúl. I had it bad for José. Real bad. Like the kind of bad that keeps a middle school girl up late at night in her bedroom sweating.

Secret Keeper

Anyway, José, Raúl, and I traveled together to different competitions. We usually rode the bus and sat together. Sometimes, a girl named Jasmine teamed up with Raúl, so I'd have José all to myself. Jasmine behaved like a bumblebee, flying here, there, and everywhere. Talking. Always talking. Her skin matched the tires on the bus we rode, and Raúl's matched the cream that goes in coffee. Cream and coffee, they nestled up together while José and I talked.

Riding home from a late-evening competition, I squished in beside José and snuggled up close. Not too close, but close. I didn't want to appear *desperate*! I wanted to be chosen; I helped him make his choice. I snuggled in close and leaned my head against José's shoulder. Nothing. He did nothing. He talked to me like normal, telling me about the competition and this car he wanted, a girl he spoke to in math class, and how his momma always forced him to eat more and more. Typical.

A few weeks later, he noticed me. I mean, really noticed me. In middle school, getting noticed might be good, or it might be bad. If an adult noticed me, I wanted to crawl back into a cocoon. If they complimented me, I might flap my butterfly wings just once. But when a boy noticed me, I flapped those wings, spilling my fairy dust everywhere, all over that boy. Not desperately. I had standards. Anyway, walking down the hall, José noticed me.

The weekend prior, we'd had dinner together: Raúl, José, Jasmine, and I. We sat outside the school on the grass and ate a picnic dinner of school-made bologna sandwiches, diced pears, and chocolate milk—in a box, of course. When we finished, one of our directors walked by and told us to huddle together for a picture. José huddled in tightly against me. My hands clammed. The starfish came out, pulling me toward the ground. Beads of sweat ran down my back.

Click. The camera flashed and before my eyes recovered from the swirling halos, José peeled himself away and carried his garbage to the can. He threw my hopes away too. Until he noticed me in the hallway.

I lifted my head up when he called my name. "Shree, Shree!"

Yes, your majesty! Anything you desire right away.

"Hey, José."

"Hey, girl, how you been?"

"Good. You?"

I knew he'd blurt out, "I been missing you, girl. You so fly. Why don't you let me drape my arm around you, and then walk down these halls with me, Sugar?"

Instead, he said, "I forgot about you until I saw you in the hallway. Girl, you awesome!" Then he punched me in the shoulder. He didn't wrap his arm around my shoulder; he punched me in the shoulder. Like I was a boy.

Homeboy

Just like in elementary school, I became the homeboy. In elementary, I played with the boys all the time. I could outrun, outjump, and out-tetherball most of them. They loved having me on their team for tag or kickball. They never wanted me as their girlfriend. Just their friend. As a cute little girl, I didn't understand. I played with Barbie, loved Hello Kitty, and dressed cutely like the other girls. I also ran faster and kicked harder. Like the homeboys.

I got the picture. When my hands clammed up and the starfish emerged, rejection loomed around the corner. With his big bug eyes, cocking his head like a rooster. Waiting. Waiting for me to give my heart away, and then *BAM!* He'd whack it. I became the homeboy.

I hung out with José and Raúl, but I showed no interest. I showed interest in their stories and their laughter, cars, and girls, but I showed no interest in being their girl. And they were just fine with that.

Then along came Michael, the most beautiful boy I'd ever seen. At least in middle school. We'd moved out of our home with my actual stepfather, Otis, back near the Jordan Downs projects, and the poverty set in. We hadn't embarked on our full nomadic lifestyle yet, but my clothes grew less fashionable, and our home grew less stable and more infested. After I moved, I walked with a new group of boys—I wasn't the homeboy anymore. And along came Michael.

Michael sat next to me in history class. His hair looked like he trimmed it every day and dyed it with the night sky. His eyebrows formed two perfect arches over even darker eyes, and his smile melted the ice off the air conditioner hanging out of the classroom window. Yes, we had an air conditioner in that class, although I am sure the premenopausal teacher brought it from her home. Judging by her mood swings, the air conditioning stood between us and a gremlin. I'd cross my legs and swing my feet and gaze at Michael, content to live in a frozen classroom with a Gila monster for him.

Michael smelled like—like—like—*ah!* There used to be a soap commercial jingle that rang, "You're not fully clean unless you're Zestfully clean." Michael walked up behind me, tapped me on the shoulder, saponified, and zestfully washed over me. I had an Herbal Essence moment right there.

"Hey, Re. You wanna hang out after school?"

"Sure! Where do you want me to meet you?"

The starfish emerged. My back got sweaty. He smiled. Another Herbal Essence moment.

"At the field."

What field? You mean under the bleachers at the football field, or locked in the closet next to the concession stand by the football field?

"What field, Michael?"

"The soccer field. Behind the school."

All day I dreamed of meeting Michael on the field and how we would do the cha-cha down the fifty-yard line. Or at least hold hands. I knew I needed something and something real. I needed a good lie. I'd be home late, so I needed a good lie for Momma. And for Michael. What excuse could I give Momma for staying after school? Cadet season was over. I hadn't joined the drama club yet.

After school, I raced from my class to the soccer field. I beat Michael by nine minutes, but who was counting? The back door burst open, the sun gleamed into the dark hallway illuminating his shadowy figure, and out walked . . . Jorge. *Jorge? What's Jorge doing here instead of Michael? Wait, here comes José? Charles. Sergio.*

Five other boys walked onto the field before Michael arrived, but who counted? I crossed my arms and bit my lip. He bounded up to me, wafting over me with that clean scent, and said, "What's wrong, Re?"

"I thought you wanted to meet *me* out here."

"I did want to meet you out here. We are short a player."

"You asked me to play soccer?"

"Yeah. I play soccer every day after school. I thought you knew. Look, Re, you my homeboy, and I thought you'd make it fun. But if you don't wanna play . . ."

I played. I wore a white, flowing skirt that day, but I had shorts on underneath, so I played anyway. By the time we finished playing, I'd skinned my knees and grass-stained my skirt. But Michael didn't smell like *ah!* anymore. He smelled like *uh!*

"Shree, you the best girl a dude could ever know, you know that? You awesome. You my homeboy."

He put his arm around me and pulled me in tight, up against his armpit. I nearly cried. I couldn't get the smell out of my nose for the next twenty minutes.

I walked home with the guys but turned a few streets early so they wouldn't see where I lived. Both my knees were scabbed over with blood, and I straightened my skirt. When I walked through the door, Momma stood there, that look in her eye.

"Where you been, child?"

"I was helping them work the concession stand for a football game." It was March, so I got my butt beat that night. *Ah! To be home, boy!*

Chosen

José punched me in the arm, Michael kicked me with the ball, and Lafayette hit me in the gut. But Lafayette also placed within me the desire to be chosen like the most valuable drop of water in the ocean. Like he chose Wanette.

Chosen like the belle of the ball.

Secret Keeper

Understand

My experience reading this chapter was

Shree Walker

Ring My Belle

One more dance and I'll be chosen. I'll be the belle every guy wished he had chosen. I'd tell myself that over and over, the visions of Lafayette dancing through my memory. So what? A middle school girl dreams about boys, right? What's the big deal? I suppose there isn't a big deal until she sells herself on a lie about boys. A lie such as being a secret makes me special.

    We moved again during middle school, so I had to start over. A new school, a new cadet team, a new boy. I wanted to impress a boy named Marcos. He had a sister named Cynthia in the same grade, who had dark flowing hair and bright eyes. Marcos and Cynthia had the same dad, but different mothers, and Marcos was only two months older. They also had two other siblings. All three adults and all four kids lived together. Don't ask me.

    Marcos's good looks preceded him. The girls swooned after him, but if any got too close, Cynthia took care of that. Like a cat-crazed girlfriend, she threatened to scratch the eyes out of any girl who tried to get with Marcos. Any girl, that is, except for me. Cynthia and I became tight. When she blew like fire, I smothered like water. And when I blew like fire, she smothered like water. We balanced each other, like Yin and Yang—and Marcos on the side running through my mind. Or dancing.

Marcos could dance. Boy, could he move. Cynthia too, but nothing like Marcos. He had slippery hips and quick feet, but his eyes moved the best. The second-to-last dance I attended in middle school featured Marcos and everybody else. At the time, Cynthia and I danced together, and I'd laid eyes on Marcos, but I hadn't laid hands on him yet.

I asked Cynthia if she'd mind if I danced with Marcos, and she told me, "No problem." Marcos and I danced a few songs together, never touching, but we had fun. Then the starfish returned. I had to get away. After too much punch and too little recovery time, I made my way to the restroom.

Middle school restrooms have their own section in dirty hell. Dirty girls make dirty comments about dirty boys and their dirty hands, all while the toilets, floors, and sinks are dirty. I slipped through the doorway, no doors on the hinges, not in middle school, no way, and bumped into Penelope. Mean girls feared Penelope. I didn't fear Penelope, but I couldn't pee with other girls in the restroom.

Penelope and the other girls stole some cigarettes and took turns puffing. I couldn't wait any longer, so I said, "Excuse me," and pushed by. I locked the stall up, wiped it down, said my prayers, and hovered a few inches above the seat, waiting. Waiting, waiting, waiting, and the girls went quiet. I knew huge wads of nasty, wet paper towels would be raining down on my head at any moment, but I couldn't hold it any longer. Or let it go.

Finally, I heard Penelope call, "You got stage fright?"

"Uh-huh."

The other girls laughed. I heard the water come on in the sink, and I reached to pull up my panties when Penelope called, "Yeah, I get it too." She marched out of the restroom and the girls followed.

Relief.

When I returned to the dance, both Cynthia and Marcos had been dragged out by a principal. Apparently, some girl got too close to Marcos and got cat scratch fever.

Shree Walker

Kiss and Tell

In the meantime, before I laid hands on Marcos, I had developed a lying streak. I'd never considered myself to be an outright liar, but I did a pretty good job lying to myself. And to Momma. I didn't like coming home after school, so I'd tell Momma I stayed late for this club or that club or this practice, or whatever. Sometimes I lied about what I watched on TV or where I got some money. Sometimes I lied about where I went.

I'd ride the city bus and take it on the 115 all the way down to the beach on the weekends. I made up excuses for Momma, like "I was playing hopscotch at the park"—at twelve years old!

I met this boy, Kenny, on the city bus. Loud as hell, let me tell you, Kenny was loud as hell on the bus. And on the street. At the beach and in school. Oddly, I met Kenny on the bus, but we attended the same school.

Hanging with Kenny always led to some type of excitement. One time he stole a kid's bike right out of the kid's hands and rode away. He only rode around the block and brought it back to the kid, but it created enough crazy to make everyone feel on edge. Safe, but near danger.

Kenny played it cool. We talked. We flirted. We met at school and walked the halls together. I shared my first-ever kiss with him on the bus. Then we followed it up by making out in the stairwells. He'd try to touch me, but I'd push his hands down. Lips only.

I played it safe, right on the edge. Soon, Kenny broke up with me and chased some girl who would put out. He never chose me. He used me. Before Kenny, I didn't want boys being physically affectionate toward me—other than hugging me—because I associated physical affection with abuse. With Kenny, I learned that letting boys touch me made me special. I didn't have to be a secret all the time. Maybe they'd choose me if they could touch me.

Heaven and Hell

I went to church with Grandmama to find the spirit. Something empty crawled inside me, and I didn't like it. I felt the void increasing. The gnawing. Church filled the void for the moment. Grandmama and I went together and listened to the preacher.

Church was different. People there treated me kindly, spoke to me, made me feel welcome and accepted. Like a parallel world, I escaped to church to get away from the world, but I didn't take any of the church back with me into the world.

One Sunday, the preacher preached about our bodies. He said something about our bodies being temples of the Holy Spirit, so we ought not to go around passing them out like candy. He told us to avoid the booty trap. Everyone laughed, but I didn't. I had never thought of my body as a temple of anything. I'd been touched by dirty hands, so my body seemed more like a tent. Used. I had protected my tent because my childhood made me feel violated.

After listening to his sermon, I wanted to protect it again. No problem. No boys wanted to put their hands on me anyway. I was still the homeboy.

Belle of the Ball

The springtime sun peeked through the blinds at Momma's house as I dressed. That night, that Saturday night, we had the last middle school dance, the last dance of eighth grade. They called it the Mardi Ball. And I was invited.

No, nobody asked me to the ball, but Cynthia wanted to know if I was going. Yeah, I was going. One more ball, and I might score me a handsome prince. Like her brother Marcos.

I dressed my temple. The family scrounged together enough money and bought this burgundy ballroom dress with wide straps that came over the shoulders and tapered to a *V* on my chest, then blossomed into a fantastic bow on one side. That dress may be the most beautiful thing I owned in my childhood. I primped and posed and prepared. Momma did my hair in the kitchen—where else? I felt so pretty. Momma snapped pictures.

Momma dropped me at the dance, and Cynthia and I snapped pictures together. We pulled in Marcos and some other friends too. Starfish emerged.

The night felt magical, and I knew the belle would break her cocoon and sprinkle her fairy dust soon. Cynthia and I danced together. Not only did Cynthia talk sassy, but she also danced sassy. She grabbed her dress with her hands and whipped it back and forth with her hips. That girl could move too. Some boy dragged her away. She kept one eye on Marcos and one eye on the boy. I kept both eyes on Marcos.

The night wore on. I danced with a few boys who were my friends during my short time at the school. None of them asked me to dance or pursued me or chose me, but they wanted to dance with me. They gave me a kind of look, and then we chatted and danced. But none of them looked at me the way Lafayette looked at Wanette so long ago in my mind. Until Marcos.

Marcos stared across the room, pulling me with those eyes. He danced, sliding his hips around like cymbals crashing into the night sky. I lusted. I wanted to guard my temple, but for just a moment, I wanted it to be dirty again.

Marcos danced toward me, looking at me as Lafayette had looked at Wanette. He smiled as he slipped up close. "Shree, do you want to dance?"

"Yes!"

"Then where is she?"

"Who?"

"Cynthia. Where is Cynthia?"

"Cynthia? Oh. Yeah. She's over there."

Marcos walked by. I never laid hands on him.

At the end of the night, Cynthia and Marcos walked out together. Before leaving, she ran over and gave me a quick hug. Marcos, when he reached the door, gave me a half-hearted wave at Cynthia's prompting. Always an afterthought.

The belle of the ball died that night. She pretended to have fun and feel excited, but she expired. I had a quick funeral, a shallow grave, and drive-by internment. I threw a few shovels of dirt on top.

Beauty didn't get the boys. Being one of the boys didn't get the boys. What did Wanette have that I didn't?

Nothing. That's when it hit me. Lafayette had a conversation with me across the room without using words. We used our eyes. We used our eyes to communicate our desire, and he did so with his girlfriend standing next to him. I *had* been chosen. It was our little secret. He noticed me. Being a secret, being noticed, being chosen meant giving yourself to a man on his terms, especially if he had someone else. That made it more special. Lafayette chose me; he communicated it with his eyes.

Analyze

After reading this chapter, I feel

Shree Walker

Illicit Love

"When dealing with people, remember you are not dealing with creatures of logic, but creatures of emotion."
– Dale Carnegie

Why try to elicit love when you can illicit love? I had four thought monsters: the fear monster (Pain), the trust monster (Doubt), the inadequacy monster (Perfectionism), and the unworthy monster (Loneliness). My childhood reinforced the existence of these monsters. They owned me—I could not escape.

Those thought monsters chased me throughout my adolescence and into my adulthood. I built some fences, some defense mechanisms, to protect me from the thought monsters. One slipped by my defenses and planted an ever-present thought: dangerous love exceeds safe love. Illicit love stirred deeper emotions than eliciting love. Eliciting love took work and often ended in rejection. Illicit love intoxicated. Like any drug, it did its job, and I got high.

One of the ten core beliefs I incorporated to defend against the thought monsters is Core Belief #8: I Have Meaningful Engagements with Myself and Others. *I forgot about myself.* The insidious lie that being a secret made me special led me to ignore my appointments with myself and to keep them with other people—the people who kept me a secret. Being a secret made me stupid, and not just for a little while.

Blocked

I blocked Leon out of my life. He slipped up and left me unprotected, so I blocked him, and I received a great reward in return. I got back my blocks of time. I blocked out time for me. I made time to exercise, read, go to counseling, engage in furthering my education, etc. As the queen, I reemerged as the most important person in my castle. As long as I kept him blocked.

Free to make appointments with myself, and free to keep appointments with myself, I felt free. Sure, I enjoyed the love and the lust, but I wanted to improve, move on, be true to myself. I wanted to experience life fully. I wanted to be a true expression of myself. I wanted to be me. I wanted to stop missing Leon. I wanted to unblock him. I wanted to be a secret again. I wanted to be special.

Back at It

I have a mind-numbing ability to learn the same lesson repeatedly. Lies do that. They return stronger, and my overwhelming persuasive power to persuade myself evolves into a highly performing mechanism that inspires awe. I call it "lying to myself, so I can do what I want anyway."

So we were right back at it. Leon walked out of a grocery store near my place—I had a sneaking suspicion as to why he was shopping near my place—and he spotted me.

Leon called out. "Hey, I been trying to call you. Why aren't you answerin' my calls."

"Oh my gosh! Why are you hobbling around on crutches?"

"Tore my ACL."

"How'd you do that?"

"How do you think?"

"Soccer."

"Yeah. Some guy tripped me, and I tore it. I've been on crutches for a few months now. Had surgery two months ago. Dark time."

"What do you mean?"

"I couldn't get out. I felt locked up. Like I was in prison. Why haven't you answered my calls?"

"You messed up. You left your phone out for your girlfriend, and you left me exposed."

"You know she took it when I wasn't around."

"What I know is I protected you, but you didn't protect me."

"What I know is, you like it a little dangerous—"

"You're right."

"How's your camping?"

"Good. I've been camping in the living room a lot lately."

"You still like your place with a tent set up right in the middle?"

"Yeah."

"But . . ."

"It gets lonely."

"How about I come over tonight and check it out?"

"In your condition? You can't even bend over to crawl in there."

"You can help me."

"Yeah. I can."

And we were right back at it. Leon came over that night, and we ate dinner together. I made ziti, changed his bandages, and helped him in and out of the shower. He never looked at my tent. I guess time got away from us, and we were so free together that we didn't notice.

I didn't need to make appointments with myself. He needed me. I needed to keep my schedule open for him. I couldn't send him home to the witch. How would he handle it being bored, stuck, lonely? If she loved him, he wouldn't need to run over here to me. I'd help him. Nurse him back to strength. Just for a little while. He'd recover, and I'd block him again. I'd get my time blocks back then.

In the future, once he recovered and I could block him again, I'd pay attention to myself and keep my promises to myself, but he needed me. This time would be different. I always said, "I'd treat others like I wanted to be treated," and he needed me. If I were injured, I'd want someone to help me, so I had to help him. I didn't need to keep appointments with myself. He needed me.

Truth Expressed

I knew the truth, and the truth had set me free. Leon came over every night of the week. He spent four to six hours at my home nightly.

"How'd your appointment with the orthopedic go today?"

"Good. Really good. How about your appointment with the doctor? How's your blood pressure?"

"It's been kind of high lately. I seem to be quite anxious all the time, but I'm not sure why. I am so free with you."

"I know. I wanted to talk to you about that."

"About what?"

"About helping me out with something. My mom, you know she's back in South America, and she's getting up in years. Not feeling as good, can't take care of herself and all that."

"And . . ."

"I want to move her here."

"What's that got to do with being free?"

"You know. I don't feel free at home. I don't want my mother right down the street from my house, checking up on me. I've already got that."

"So what do you want?"

"I want to move her to this side of town. Over here. By you."

"I don't know if that's a good idea."

"She needs someone to look after her, and I'll be able to come check on her when I come see you."

"Yes, I'd like that. You'll be around more. But won't you have to explain to your mom what you're always doing on this side of town? What if she sees us together?"

"I can't have friends on this side of town? I'll be coming over here to check on her. She'll appreciate it."

"Appreciate what?"

"All the attention."

"Can I meet her?"

"You don't think I want to introduce her to you? I want her to meet you. Hell, I want the two of you to become friends. She'll love you. You can talk music and all that with her."

"What about her?"

"Who?"

"Your girl."

"She don't know. I don't tell her nothing. She won't want Momma to come. She'd be afraid I'd listen to Momma and not her."

"Do you listen to her anyway?"

"I listen to myself—and you. You help me out with my problems. My taxes, my daughter. She can't even talk about art or music with me. She's boring."

"You really want me to meet your Momma? You ain't scared?"

"Of Momma? Course not."

"No, I mean of Momma figuring it out."

"She knows. She knows a man can't be bored and lonely. He needs a soulmate, someone to talk to. My girlfriend ain't it. She's the mother of my child, and that's it. She's not like you. We belong together, tell each other everything. You get me. She doesn't."

"You still want to travel, see the world? How are you going to do that with your elderly mom here?"

"I'll see it. I'll take you with me sometimes. Momma don't mind. I just want to protect her here, get her out of that place, you know? She'll want to go back and visit. And I'll go with her. I can travel all over South America when I'm down there. I still haven't seen Chile or been up to Tobago. There's places I want to see."

"You can't do that now when you visit her?"

"Not as much when I go to see her. When I take her, that's different. She'll see her people. I'll travel. Maybe take you."

"So you askin' or you tellin'?"

"Both. I got you something."

"Huh?"

"I got you something. Here, open it."

He handed me a white box, rectangular, the size of a sheet of paper, and it had gold letters emblazoned on the top. I didn't even look at it.

"No, I can't take this."

"Open it."

"No, I can't. Really. Well, I guess I can give it one little peek."

"Open it. You'll see."

I opened the box. Inside lay the most beautiful necklace I'd ever seen. Several jade stones encircled in gold dazzled my eyes. I imagined how it would look around my neck, dangling near my neckline. Before I could thank him, Leon took the box from me.

"Here. Let me put it on."

"Now?"

"Right now."

I turned. He shimmied up behind me, pushing his crutches out of the way. He reached around, draped it over my neck, pushing in tight, and latched it in the back. I turned.

"It's beautiful. You know, they say the girl makes the dress, but you make the necklace. It looks so much better on you."

"I love it!"

I walked to the mirror and gazed at the necklace, eyes wide. The dragon stared back, but all I saw was the princess, the little girl who'd been denied being noticed. I smiled.

"There's earrings too."

"What?"

"You didn't see? In the box there. Jade earrings too. See?"

"I love them! I love you."

"I love you too."

"You know, with you, I can say that and truly mean it. You're the only man I've met I can be myself with. I don't know what I'd do without you."

"I don't know what I'd do without you."

"I hated our time apart. I missed you every day."

"I missed you too. Let me see that necklace!"

"Come get it."

Being a secret made me special. Meeting his Momma would make me their secret.

No More Lies

Leon said, "I hate liars."

"What are you talking about?"

"Liars, man, I hate 'em. I work with this one dude; he lies all the time. I get it. It's part of the job and all, but he lies about nonsense. You know, like, 'What you get into last night?' and he be like, 'Man you know I was at the strip club last night, tearin' it up. Ladies drapin' themselves all over me. You know how I do.' Then I talk to his boy, and they were sittin' up, whining about their wives last night. He didn't go to no strip club. Why didn't he just say he chilled at the house? Nobody cares!"

"So why do you lie then?"

"I don't lie to you. Just to her. I don't lie to you."

"You don't lie to me?"

"Never. You ask where I've been. I tell you. I say I'm coming over, I come over. No lie."

"No lie, huh?"

"No lie. When have you caught me lying?"

"I haven't. I don't lie to you either."

"I hate liars."

"Me too. Let's promise never to lie to each other."

"I don't need to promise. I don't lie to you."

"Promise?"

"Yeah. Promise."

Secret Keeper

Evaluate

Before reading this chapter, I thought

After reading this chapter, I now think

Shree Walker

No More Lies

I put the Trust monster and the Unworthy monster back in my pocket. They were lies from my childhood. They had no power over me; I'd come too far. Who goes through all that hell just to be mediocre? Leon and I didn't lie to each other, so Doubt and Loneliness took a hike. All the way to my back pocket.

We didn't lie to each other. We made a promise, and I keep my promises.

Date Night!

"Meet me at Amerigo at seven."
"You sure? Isn't that a little close to home?"
"Nah. She don't come over to West End much. Don't worry about it. Wear the necklace."
"I will."

I love dates . . . but we didn't date much. He came over a lot, though, and we stayed up talking and laughing and eating at my place. We went out sometimes, here and there, different bars and music venues, but not too much. Most times, we sat at my place and knitted our souls together. We talked about everything: life, kids, politics, work, my students, his daughter, education, philosophy, everything. I formed a bond with this man I'd never known. I knew him better than he knew himself, better than I knew myself. I loved him, and I loved dates. I went all out.

I slipped on a red dress, blazingly red. I put on red stilettos so tall I could nearly touch the ceiling, and my necklace, of course, my necklace. No more masquerades; we were going out that night! I have this perfume I wear only for special occasions. When I smell it, I just want to die. It's so good. I sprayed myself with it.

I don't know why I got so worked up for this date. I went out all the time, and seriously, this date was casual, considering some of the places I've been and the people I've met.

I've put on many red dresses and many red lipsticks. But for Leon, I put on my best. Staying at my place seemed boring, and I did not want to be boring. Secrets aren't boring, anyway.

I arrived early, but I didn't mind. I wanted to get out and see Nashville in the fall. The red and orange trees, the smell of fall in the air, and the sights and sounds beckoned me. I'd spent too much time indoors with school and Leon. I caught some stares on the way in. Overdressed? More like dressed to kill. I didn't care.

I ordered a table for two and got a drink. I took the liberty of ordering his drink too. Rum and Coke for him, always. When the waiter brought the drinks and my salad, I ordered dinner: ziti, family style. Leon could eat, and I knew he loved ziti. My ziti. I figured Amerigo could pull a close second, which they did, and their breadsticks were awesome!

Leon showed up and strutted in, his first day without crutches. He stared at me. I waited. He traced my face with his eyes, stopped at my necklace, smiled, pulled out his chair, and said, "Wow! Mama, you look incredible tonight."

"Hey, boy. You know I dressed like this for you."

"Yeah, I see you wore the necklace I bought you."

"You know I love you."

"I love you too."

Shree Walker

Marriage

I thought about marriage. Far-fetched ideas don't scare me. I believed in the possibilities. I had a monogamous relationship with a man who had a girlfriend. So what? She was a witch. He'd leave her for me. I shook the cobwebs from my head.

Where was he anyway? The ziti grew cold. I didn't want to sit there all night imagining our life together. Where was he? 7:30. I texted him. "Hey, you on your way?" 7:45. Cold ziti on the plate. "Did you mean 8:00?" 8:00. Another round of breadsticks for the lady. "Le, I can't wait all night." 8:15. More wine. More bread. Nobody. "Le, I know you ain't comin' now, but can you tell me if you're all right?" 8:30.

"Ma'am, that gentleman over there picked up your check. You don't need to pay."

"Which gentleman?"

The waiter pointed his long finger at a red-haired man leaving his table, walking out of the restaurant with what appeared to be his wife and kids. Appeared to be. Who knew anymore?

Chatter

"You lied to me."
"I didn't lie to you. She got sick. I had to stay home."
"You couldn't text?"
"She'd see me on my phone."
"Never stopped you before."
"This was different. She was vomiting everywhere. I thought we'd end up in the hospital."
"She's fine now?"
"Yeah. At home. Look, I didn't lie to you, baby. I don't lie to you."
"Promise?"
"Yeah. Promise."

A few weeks later, I got a text from one of my friends who knew about Leon and me. "Shree, you heard about Leon?"

"What's up?"

"He's getting married."

"Married. To her? He don't even like her."
"Check it out. I'm not lying."
Of course not. Nobody lied.
I called him.
"Hey. The streets is talkin'."
"Yeah, what's that?"
"About you getting married."
"I'm not getting married. That's bull—"
"Don't lie to me."
"I don't lie to you. I told you. We made a promise. I keep my promises. I hate liars anyway. I'm comin' over."
"You're comin' over? When?"
"Now. I can't leave you like this. I'll be there in thirty minutes."
"I'm still at school. I won't be home."
"I'll be there waiting when you get there."
And he was. This time, I didn't daydream anything. When I got home, he stood beside his car, waiting for me. And spent most of the night. It was just chatter. Two weeks later, he took me to a dealership and had me sit in an Aston Martin.
"One day, you'll have one just like this."
"I know I will."
"I love you, girl."
"I love you too."

Marriage for Real

I kicked the Trust monster and Unworthy monster to the curb. Doubt and Loneliness had no place in my life anymore. Maybe I'd be a wife-to-be soon. Leon and I spent so much time together. I almost forgot that lie about him marrying her. Why would he marry her? He spent 75 percent of his time with me, anyway. People make up the dumbest chatter. Always trying to start something to keep their lives interesting. It bothered me, but I didn't have trust issues.

He made the date up to me several times over the next few months. We spent the holidays together. Of course, not the actual days because I didn't want to take him from his daughter. He went to visit his mom. He decided not to move her to Nashville. He said she liked it where she was too much. Her friends and family lived there, and she would die there. He didn't want to fight his Momma. I didn't blame him. I didn't get to meet her, but we planned for me to go the next time. There was a wedding to plan before that.

I texted him on a Friday night because he said he'd be over by six, and by seven, he hadn't arrived. He was never late. Something was up. He told me he might be a few minutes late, but an hour? Typically, he spent Friday nights at home, but he wanted to come over, and I loved it.

I received a text: "Why you texting my man again?"

What? This again? How did his girl get his phone this time? This fool was always leaving his phone around. Before, I never got a text from her on his phone, but this was the third time in the past year. Here we go.

"He asked me to review a presentation he has to give. That's it."

"We're getting married. I don't want you messing with my husband. We don't need a three-way."

"You're getting married?"

"Yes. Next month, bitch."

I called his phone.

"Why are you stalking my man?"

"I'm not stalking your man."

"He said that you won't leave him alone. He's been done talkin' to you for a few months now, but you won't stop calling and texting him."

"A few months? He was here two nights ago."

"No, he wasn't."

"You remember when he called you on Wednesday, said he had that presentation he was working on late? He was sitting on my couch when he called. You remember Tuesday when you called, and he said he had to help a buddy fix his car? Right here. You didn't notice when he came home wearing his blue, pin-striped shirt and slacks? Didn't think anything of him working on a car in nice clothes?"

"You're a loose homewrecker."

"No. I didn't know you were getting married. You may not want to believe this, but he didn't tell me that. He's been here five or six days a week for the past two months. You need more information?"

Click.

Secret Keeper

I called back. "What? The truth hurt too much to hear it? You don't wanna know your man is sneaking over here every night of the week? You just don't want to face that he don't love you. You just wanna call me names and throw stuff up in my face."

"Leave my man alone."

"I'm not chasin' your man. He comes to me."

"I've seen the texts. You're always begging him to come over. Leave him alone. If he wanted you, he'd marry you. He chose me."

"You're delusional." I hung up.

I called his other phone. He didn't answer. I drove to his office, and surprisingly, he was there.

"You told me you weren't getting married!"

"What are you talking about?"

"I talked to your girl. Why don't you keep your phone with you? What the hell did you leave it at the house for? Were you hoping to get caught?"

"What's wrong with you?"

"I talked to your girl. She said you're getting married. Why would you marry her anyway? You practically live with me!"

"I owe her. She's been with me for over a decade. If we separate, she gets my stuff too."

"No she doesn't! Tennessee doesn't even honor common-law marriages. You're not even a good liar."

"Some courts do. The state doesn't, but—why am I telling you all this anyway? Yes, we're getting married. You knew I had a girl from the beginning."

"But you told me you weren't getting married. You lied to me! You made a promise!"

"I couldn't help it. You wouldn't see me if you knew I was married. I didn't want to lose you."

"Well, you did!"

"Shree! Shree! Come back here."

I drove away in a hailstorm of emotions, crying and snorting all the way. I rushed home, locked myself back in the castle, and slayed the dragon. No more. No more lies. No more cheating. No more secrets. No more Leon. No more.

Shree Walker

One More

I needed more. I needed more validation. But not from Leon. I blocked him, deleted him, eradicated him from my memory. No, I needed more love. Not more secrets. So I dated. I dated around and met some nice men. Some very nice and interesting men. They weren't Leon, but they weren't taken either. I even invited a few of them back in. Doubt and Loneliness became my new bedfellows, and we made love every night.

    Nobody noticed. Nobody cared. I had seen the truth, and I asked it to let me be. Just one more night.

Secret Keeper

Create

After reading this chapter, I will restore myself by

Shree Walker

Truth

The addiction to the lies became my truth. Leon got married. I let him go. I moved on, content to leave the past in the past, buried alive. Like I do.

The truth is I can't leave no damned lies back in the past. I carry them around with me, nurturing them, feeding them my soul until they swallow me whole. I am not holy. I am wholly disqualified because I became addicted to the lies.

Right Back at It . . . Again

> "I ain't messin' with no married man."
> "Girl, you know that don't make no difference."
> "You lied to me!"
> "You like it spicy. If it ain't dangerous, you ain't in it."
> "You're right."

Leon and I later rekindled our illicit love affair, and this time we destroyed his marriage bed—together. He'd made a public promise to his wife; we killed it in private. He'd vowed to be true; we made it false. He made her his wife; I made her a victim. No longer would the witch win; the queen would. I looked in the mirror each day, the dragon emerging, the little girl crumbling, and I didn't care. I didn't care. What mattered was me.

We continued dating. I didn't want to know about or hear about his wife anymore. She became taboo. He stayed with me. Came to my house. Ate my dinner. Slept in my bed. Who was she? I'd been good long enough, keeping away from him, honoring their marriage. If he didn't honor it, why should I?

I should have because I don't chase environments; I change them. In this situation, I made the environment hell. If a woman can't trust her man, she doesn't have a man; she has a boy. If a woman helps a man be a boy, she's a pedophile. I participated in destroying a marriage, a man, a woman, a child, and a dream. This dragon definitely had a forked tongue.

That Girl

I continued working at Jere Baxter Alternative School and managing twilight school, teaching young boys to be men by day and a man to be a boy by night. The duplicity in my life sickened me. Addiction consumed. I lied. I believed the lies. I convinced myself of the darkness. My light did not shine; it died.

One of the gentlemen I had the privilege of working with at that time helped me. A white, Christian man, he looked like he had stepped out of Pleasantville and into the alternative school. His tie synched tightly to his neck, the creases in his pants could shave paper, and his sweater vests had no fuzz. Zero. Not one piece.

"Good morning, Ms. Walker. How are you this fine morning? Isn't it delightful to be here today?" He'd say that every single morning. Every single morning. At times, he'd try to be funny. "I suppose we're doing a great job. We're stamping out ignorance, one student at a time." He tried. Although we lived in two different worlds, he spoke to me, and his words had weight. So much weight.

I'm not much of a secret keeper because my life is more like an open book. That's why I told him about my relationship with Leon. I couldn't keep it any longer. I'd promised myself that I would be honest with myself, and that promise warred against the lie I was living.

"Look, I didn't want to do it. I didn't want to mess with a married man. I believe in the sanctity of marriage. I believe the two become one flesh, but in this case, we are tied together at the soul. With this guy, I am the freest expression of myself."

"So, you've become that girl."

"What girl?"

"The one who lies to herself."

"I'm not lying to myself. That's how I feel."

"No, Shree. That's who you are. That girl."

Caught Red-Handed

An ancient concept in horticulture promises if one spreads manure, the produce will grow. I needed that message. I needed to stop shoveling shit all over my garden, so the lies would stop growing. Then I needed to take out the hoe and hack up all the weeds. I could replant the garden so it would grow correctly.

But gardening isn't that simple. Neither is addiction. Step one meant facing the fact that I loved the lies, the secrets, the illicit love—which is not love at all. I did that. But the garden also produced good fruit: love, compassion, sympathy. I allowed the weeds to grow, and the fruit turned rotten. I used the good for evil.

I slowly cut Leon out of my life. I didn't eradicate him as I hoped, but I slowly scaled back . . . back . . . back. He didn't get it. Not all the time. I explained; he whined. Sometimes I gave in. Sometimes I stood strong.

I eventually moved in with a friend to create a barrier to help myself stand strong. I told Leon that he couldn't come over. I couldn't entertain him there. I cried at nights over the loss, over the relationship, over my self-centeredness. *Why aren't you good enough? Why can't you be chosen?* The crying didn't change the truth. I'd been messing with a married man—and the hen came home to roost.

But I didn't learn that quickly. A friend overseas needed some help, and Leon could help her. She contacted Leon, and he helped get my friend's business situated for when she returned to the States, but it came at a great cost. I got caught again, red-handed.

"I've got your money," I texted him for my friend who had asked me if I could help her out by making the payment. "I'll bring it to you tomorrow."

The next morning, I got a text from his wife's number. Apparently, she'd been checking on him and saw my text message.

"We don't want your money. Stay away from my man!"

"I'm not trying to be with your man."

"Can't you keep your own man?"

"I'm only trying to pass money from one friend to the next. I have no interest in Leon."

"Bullshit."

I called his phone. "Look. I am sorry. I am sorry for what I've done. I'm not messing with your man. I am stuck in the middle. I have a friend—"

"We don't need your money! I told you to stay away! What the hell's wrong with you anyway? Can't get your own man? Can't get one who'll stick around?"

"I told you. I don't mess with Leon anymore. I am not doing that. I am just helping a friend. I don't even want to be involved. I told—"

"And I told you. We don't want any of your filthy money! Fu—"

"Hey now! Listen. I am sorry. I told you I was sorry. I don't want to be involved. I hope you and Leon have a great life together. I am just—"

"A ho?"

"Why would I lie to you? I didn't lie the three of four times I was messin' with him. Why would I lie now?"

"Cause you's a filthy-ass skank."

Let me get her up off this phone.

"Your man ain't comin' home tonight."

"What?"

"He ain't comin' home tonight."

"What the hell is you—"

"He ain't comin' home tonight. I'm fuckin' him!"

Click.

Shree Walker

Damned Lies

These are the damned lies I told myself: *I can do this civilly. It's just one phone call. I'm capable of having a relationship with him that is only a friendship.* All this after emoting about how our souls were knit together and he helped me become a true expression of myself. Some true expression. I didn't like myself. I needed to take out the hoe and chop some weeds.

"Hey. You going home tonight?"

"What? You don't even say hello, Re? You just call me up and ask if I'm going home?"

"Yeah. You talked to your wife?"

"What?"

"Have you spoken to your wife?"

"No."

"Are you going home?"

"No. I'm going out. Why? You missing me?"

"No. I spoke to her. I texted you about the money, and you left your phone out again. She's mad. I got mad, lost my cool, told her you were sleeping here tonight."

"And . . ."

"And you need to go home."

"Why's that?"

"Please. Please go home tonight. Show her we don't have anything going on. Show her you can be a man of your word. You need to go home to her tonight."

"Nah. Can I come over?"

"Boy. Get off my phone."

I couldn't. I couldn't even manage to remove the weeds completely. The insidious lies dug too deep. I believed them too much and carried them in my pocket, in my spirit, for safekeeping. I have a friend who says, "You don't know you're drowning until you're drowning." It was too late. There were too many damned lies.

Pointed Increase, Gradual Decrease

When Leon and I met, our romance erupted quickly into a full-scale affair with all the taboo and shrapnel that come with it. Within weeks, he started staying over four to six nights per week. We continued on and on like that for four years.

When Leon and I called it quits, and by that, I mean when I called it quits, our romance waned slowly. The cycle remained unbroken. I am a strong Black woman, but I cry, I hurt, and I failed. Untying a knot that took years to tie didn't all fall apart in a matter of weeks or months. Even after our physical relationship ended, our emotional one didn't.

I don't see him anymore. I won't let myself. I can't. I'm not strong enough. Now I know the lies, but that doesn't mean I have conquered them. I make the appointments with myself, and I keep them, but Leon still sneaks into my mind. He disrupts my thoughts and beliefs. I dug too deeply and became enmeshed. Even now, I still speak to him occasionally over the phone. "Hey, how's your mom? How's your daughter? Your career doing all right?" That kind of stuff.

But it's not over. I don't believe that lie anymore. If I walk that path of discovery, I know I'll discover me, the me inside of me I don't want to be, the Shree in the mirror I don't want to see, the dragon staring back at me. I don't walk that path. I've taken a new path. That path led me down a new and interesting road . . . into the arms of Lily and Elizabeth.

Shree Walker

Apply

Because of my experience reading this chapter, now I will

Every Scar

"The night she touched me changed my life! I couldn't stop her, felt so violated. He'd drag me from my room to the bathroom, crying, wincing in the pain of a broken arm and broken body. I asked him to stop, but he didn't, so I counted fish. Who? The man in the green Chevy Nova. I smelled Daddy's jacket when he took me on the motorcycle, engine roaring in my ears. Sometimes, I can't breathe at night, lying awake, feeling under the bed for the monsters. Who's there? I told David I love him, but he pretended to be breaking up. I held Lia back. She screamed. I hear the echoes. I can't let it go. Why did he die? Why did her son die? I always saw trees. I dreamed trees. I want to go back home and nurture the little girl inside. She needs me."

    I sat on the couch in Elizabeth's office, words gushing out of my mouth, heralding traumatic experiences in no particular order. My eyes twitched. I tapped my leg. The words kept coming. I entered the trauma, became one with it, and I was scared.

    I had experience with therapy before I met Elizabeth, but it was different. Years prior, I sat in Lily's office, processing. Lily was a therapist. I don't know if she still is. I don't see her anymore. When I created the fiasco with Leon, I often visited Lily to process it. In the Black community, processing with a therapist means you're crazy. Maybe I was crazy. I needed help.

Lily, an older white lady, invited me into her office, the third story of a colonial mansion in Nashville. Her room smelled of lavender and eucalyptus. We practiced talk therapy. She listened; I talked. A lot. We unpacked some of my past, and we searched boldly into my future, but mostly, we dug through the past. We dug through the garden and tried to pull weeds.

All the while, I lived a duplicitous life with Leon, myself, and my faith. Lily helped me unpack it. She suggested eye movement desensitization and reprocessing (EMDR). I declined her suggestion.

If you're not Black, let me unpack. In my community, to process, I go to church, sit on the porch, share a drink, talk to my hairdresser, and accept "That's life. That's what was supposed to happen." Although some of these activities help, they never heal. Sometimes they bring a good laugh or a hangover. But never healing.

During my undergraduate program, I met with Dr. Faulkner. As a professor, he held us spellbound in class; as a mentor, he discussed my past with me in his office. As a clinical psychologist and a professor, Dr. Faulkner warranted trust. I learned to trust him during our many conversations. He helped with the Doubt monster.

Not Enough

Just like with any appetite, I'm never fully satisfied with therapy. Unless I am wholly healed. Not all wounds fully heal. The amputee is still an amputee, and I am still abused. Scars heal where wounds reside. My scars had healed, but some still hurt when touched. Some of my therapy involved reopening the old wounds, properly cleaning them out, and then sewing them back up to form new scars. New, more healed scars.

Dr. Faulkner opened my mind to therapy. I understood, with time, that therapy helped me heal. The therapy was not enough. I must face my past and my present. I must change today what I became because of yesterday. Dr. Faulkner opened my eyes, but he couldn't do the work.

Shortly thereafter, I met Lily. We dug through my past and discussed my trauma. One time she asked if I enjoyed the abuse. A bitter question, and I met it with a bitter response.

My face said, "Screw you! What the hell is wrong with you?" My mouth said, "Huh?"

"You've heard of Stockholm syndrome?"

"Yes, but what's that got to do with me?"

"Everything. Trauma. Abuse. Feelings of affection for your captor."

"No! I hated it, every minute of it."

"You never tried to protect him?"

"Yes. Yes, I did. Because the secret made me special, and I wanted to—"

"Be special. You protected him? You don't need to agree if this isn't true. Go slow. Take your time. I know it's traumatic."

"No. I wanted to protect him so he . . . this can't be my fault. I thought it was my fault, but you told me it wasn't my fault! Now you're telling me it's my fault! I don't know what to believe!"

"I'm not telling you it was your fault. I am telling you that you were traumatized, and as a result, you may have developed Stockholm syndrome. Shree, that's a normal feeling to have. It doesn't make you dirty. I'm sorry he hurt you. Tell me how you feel."

"I feel betrayed. Betrayed by my own body. What do I do?"

"Well, it sounds like you first need to accept that you were abused, and it's not your fault. You can't reach back into the past and take the blame for something that's not yours. He abused you. You were not equipped to escape. But first, you need to feel the betrayal. I'm here. It's okay to feel it. You were not equipped to escape—"

"But I—"

"Told your mother when you felt safe. Like you should have. You did exactly what you were supposed to do."

"What do I do?"

"How about EMDR?"

"What's that?"

"We use a movement that allows you to freely rehearse your experiences, so we can file them away correctly. You'll step back into your past and just let the feelings fly, for lack of a better explanation."

"No. I'm not interested for now."

"Okay. We'll do it your way."

I want to add a disclaimer. I can't explain EMDR. I'm not qualified. It's complicated and dangerous—it takes you through your full range of emotions, including the more volatile ones—although it can bring healing. I still have scars, but the EMDR helped me process through how I got them and how I can move forward. I'm not here to persuade. I'm here to tell my story.

Too Much

I often wondered why I was not enough or too much. I've struggled with that dichotomy of thought since I can remember. *Why am I not enough for Daddy, No Name, Leon? Am I too much for them? Is that my problem? Did I give up too easily? Take it too far?* Even when it came to therapy, I'd ask the same questions. *Have I had too little therapy? Too much?*

After the Leon debacle, I realized I had too much therapy. It didn't work. Much later, I realized I hadn't had too much therapy because I didn't do the required work. I didn't face my fears. I feared too much therapy would lock me in the crazy cell. Wrong. The lies locked me in the crazy cell; therapy helped me get out. Or it helped me try to escape.

Enter Elizabeth, whom I met through a mutual friend. I was in therapy when I had my affair with Leon, so I knew I needed something different. I needed someone to talk to, and I wanted to try EMDR. I wanted to do whatever I could to heal. Before I met Elizabeth, I still had reservations. Not about her, about myself. I didn't know if I could heal.

I formed trauma bonds. I had a trauma bond with No Name. I had a trauma bond with my friend Lia—her son died in a tragic automobile accident. I developed a trauma bond with my therapist Lily. Not their fault; it was mine. I wanted this time to be different. Only healing, no trauma bonds.

Elizabeth reached inside me and jiggled things around in a way Lily never would. Not in a bad way. Just different. A young, articulate, snappy white lady, Elizabeth measured as a direct antithesis to Lily. Instead of being motherly and nurturing, she bit.

"You're afraid."

"No, I'm not ready."

"Which means you're afraid. You're afraid to face your past and speak the truth. You want to speak 'your truth' so it pacifies you and seems less harsh. Speak *the* truth."

"The truth is I was sexually abused, molested, and raped. Is that good enough?"

"And you both hated and loved the men who did it."

"No."

"Yes."

"I didn't love them."

"I didn't say you loved what they did. I said you loved them. That's why the experience registers as so traumatic. An enemy hurts you, and it registers trauma. A friend betrays you, and it registers an entirely different level of trauma."

"Okay, so I loved and hated them. That's why I'm so bitter over my relationship with Leon."

"What do you mean?"

"I facilitated his betrayal. I encouraged it. I am not the victim. I am the perpetrator this time."

"Do you believe that's true?"

"Yes. I hated myself for that."

"But you didn't stop."

"I hate myself."

"Now, there's some truth. What do you do when you hate someone? How do you get past it?"

"Forgive them. I think I need to forgive myself."

"Do you think you need to be forgiven?"

"I can't entirely forgive myself. I must accept it."

"From whom do you receive forgiveness?"

"God, I guess."

"You guess."

"I know."

"Then from God."

"But what about David?"

"You made a choice."

"I gave up."

"You grew up."
"But I didn't choose the marriage."
"You chose yourself."

That wasn't the hard part! Her sessions with me pulled, pulled, pulled, and when we used EMDR, it pushed, pushed, pushed. Most people deal with an hour session of EMDR, or an hour and a half, tops. My schedule, after completing graduate school and taking a director's position, speaking part-time, and volunteering, constricted me to splurging for longer bi-weekly sessions. In other words, I attended counseling every other week for a three-hour session. *Gilligan's Island* had nothing on me.

I needed counseling from the counseling. Well, that's not true, but EMDR counseling eclipsed painful. I experienced trauma during the counseling, but I learned to file away my memories properly in their categories. I no longer carry around internal questions such as, *What did I do wrong?* Touching the scars hurt, and it still does—that's why I jump-kicked my boyfriend—but I continue my search for healing.

I am not too much or too little. I work on being the me I want to be. I make appointments with myself, and I keep them. I engage the stories in my mind and change them. I work diligently to destroy the thought monsters. They have their doubts; I have my belief. As I said, "I don't chase environments. I change them." This time for good.

Secret Keeper

Understand

My experience reading this chapter was

Nobody

I have a bone to pick. I'm not an angry Black woman, but "for everything there is a season." I'm going to start a fight.

One day I answered my phone. "This is Shree."

"Dr. Walker, how you doing?"

"Well, Anthony! How are you?"

"Good, good. Listen, I don't know what to do about these students returning from the juvenile detention centers. How do I get caught up with what they learned there?"

"Have you received the wraparound notes?"

"No. Where do I get those?"

"Check your email. You should have received them within seventy-two hours. It'll come from eschool, so it may automatically route to another folder."

"Okay, got it. What next?"

"Read the email, contact the site coordinator, and schedule the wraparound at your school. You should have a flow map on your H-drive. You should also have notes in the email that give you the contact information for the student's guardians and his or her previous school."

"Right, but how do I get them integrated into the school?"

"You'll discover that in your wraparound. Use the questionnaire at the bottom of the flow map to create a conversation with the student, and when you discover his or her interests, you're golden. Anthony?"

"Yeah."

"It's imperative they form a community within the first two weeks. If not, they'll go rogue, and you'll have more issues."

"How do I help them form a community?"

"Use the questionnaire to discover the interest. Mandate they get involved. It's part of their probationary period when returning from JDC."

"Got it."

"Anthony?"

"Yeah."

"Thanks for calling."

That conversation took place two weeks ago. I haven't worked in that district for well over two years.

Work, Works

When I began teaching, I taught on a probationary certification. I was uncertified yet I crushed it. I taught at the alternative school in harsh environments with children who needed a leader. I led. I got certified. I got promoted.

I finished graduate school, earned a doctorate, and continued teaching while I served as an administrator at twilight school. I taught day and night. I did the work. All the work. I also served as an adjunct professor at Belmont University. Doing the work, I got promoted.

As a dean of students, I created processes. The school where I served educated underprivileged students, in an underprivileged neighborhood, in an underprivileged environment. By *underprivileged*, I mean they hadn't had the privilege of having all the systems built for them.

Chaos

Kids didn't get lunch. Students jostled from their classrooms, bouncing all over the halls, yelling and fighting all the way to the lunchroom. The lines extended down the hall. In the hallway, they cornered weaker students, "pantsed" one another, and some went to the bathroom to fill the toilet with paper towels and flush it continually or to sneak drugs or sex (whichever they could get their hands on while in middle school).

Kids slugged it out. They dragged other children to the bathroom, crying, and tattooed them with aggression. Why do I call it a bathroom and not a restroom? Because nobody rested. They bathed in their own sweat, seethed in their own humiliation, and humiliated others. People say, "Kids these days have no respect." Respect wasn't the problem. These kids didn't have order.

These students had zero order. Parents pretended to parent while pacifying their children with electronics and pacifying themselves with vices. Rather than discipline, they clung to passivity or violence. Not all parents. Not all students. I'll stop right here and add this justification.

Chaos played its part in my personal life too, but not on the job. I am educated, and I am hardworking, so I did the work. At school, I did the work, and I brought order.

The lunchroom invited chaos. Pack hundreds of middle school students into any unstructured environment, and chaos ensues. But the lunchroom also provided food. And students want to eat. Make order a prerequisite for eating, and order is restored, so that's what I did.

I created a system. We separated the tables into pods, no more than four at a pod at a time. We arranged the serving lines into serving stations—throughout the lunchroom. The maximum number of students allowed at one station couldn't exceed ten. We tiered the classroom dismissal times. Students left class based on teacher dismissal, and each class was released in tiers 1–5, two minutes apart.

We removed the bathroom doors because the hinges were enough for middle school students. (The stalls still had doors.) Students could access the restroom for thirty seconds to wash their hands before lunch and had to be dismissed to the restroom during lunch.

Each student proceeded through the serving line—whether they brought a lunch or purchased a lunch—and we directed them to their seats. No, they didn't always get to sit with their friends. Yes, everybody received an entire lunch period to eat their lunch in their seats. We then permitted them to return their tray, wipe down their space, and place the chair on the table after lunch. The purpose of the lunch period was to eat, not to play. Order.

Order

I could go on and on. We created positive learning environments, met the needs of students with special needs, involved parents, the whole gamut. We created order, and as a result, I got promoted.

I worked with special populations. I have a knack for seeing a need, meeting a need, and understanding a need. I call it compassion and common sense, but it's not so common. No big deal. I have no room to judge. But I did the work and got promoted again.

As the director of special populations for over 86,000 students and over one hundred sites, responsibility found me. Like a dump truck. I loved it. I upgraded my department from two to six employees over the time I served and advocated for their benefits. My team received raises, special recognition, and the latitude to do their jobs well.

We created so many processes, and they got so many promotions, and then it all stopped.

Order Created Chaos

"What do you mean you can't reimburse me for the past two years? I've been underpaid on my salary for two years, and you can't fix it?"

"Dr. Walker, I'm terribly sorry, but we can't justify extending the budget to compensate you for time served. We can adjust your current pay to match the pay schedule approved by the board."

"But you can't adjust it to match the pay schedule approved by the board for what I've already done? It's just my loss?"

"Dr. Walker, again, we appreciate your service, but there's no protocol for reimbursing pay for time served. Only for current work."

"Then create one."

"Dr. Walker, as I've previously stated, we cannot reimburse you for time served."

A strange phenomenon occurs when order disrupts chaos. Some people hate it. Some people thrive off the chaos, and without the chaos, they cannot rely on their anxiety to propel them to "success." To ameliorate this tragic loss in their lives, the loss of hyperactivity, they panic and create chaos. When I brought order into my department and across the district, instead of gratitude, I received ignorance.

I got ignored. In my situation, when people ignored the issue, they feigned ignorance. They'd rather pretend the problem didn't exist rather than face it.

I call this feigned ignorance a "bottle cap" mentality. When I have a soda bottle, the cap keeps the soda inside the bottle. It brings order to the situation. If I don't have a bottle cap, then the soda spills. If I shake the soda up, it'll shoot out the top. The bottle cap provides the order, so I ignore I have a bottle cap because all is well. However, if I lose the bottle cap, I have a new problem—soda all over my new pants.

A bottle cap mentality ignores the fact that the bottle cap brings order to a bottle. Without the cap, the bottle is a long-nosed cup. So, a person with a bottle cap mentality looks at a full soda bottle and believes all is well. If someone removes the cap, she'll ignore it and spill soda all over her dress. Walk around with the stain saying, "It's just how bottles work. What can you do?" Does this sound like an exaggeration? Try this one: "Kids cheat. What can you do?" I don't know. Maybe put a cap on it!

The person with a bottle cap mentality just ignores what brings order to a situation! If she loses the cap, then she'll just deal because she doesn't realize the value of the cap. Thus, when the cap is on, all is well, and there's no perceived possibility for chaos. She can take the cap for granted. Maybe she'll just put a band-aid over the bottle, and all will be well.

I'm here to start a fight. I worked from the bottom to the top, changing the environments I entered, making the pathway straight, and in return, I got ignored.

Ignorance

Within the district, people respected me. I had a reputation for problem-solving. Many of my coworkers, colleagues, and direct reports treated me with respect. They respected me because I helped them, and I didn't create a sense of fear. But when I dealt with HR, I received disrespect.

"Can I have a compensation review? My department increased from two to six, and I have stretched the department from being responsible for two sectors of the district's population to six."

"I'm sorry, but that doesn't make sense."

On another occasion: "Okay, I've conducted a review of my role and responsibilities. Can we change my title or create a position that accurately reflects my position to compensate me for my duties?"

"I'm sorry. The duties you represent reflect the duties of the director of special populations."

"No, they reflect the duties of the director of special populations *now*—after I fixed the chaos and more burdens were offloaded to us so we could fix those."

"I'm sorry. You need to write a proposal listing your responsibilities and those of the department, cross-reference it with other local districts and their pay scale, and then identify why you specifically should receive compensation above what is listed for your position."

"I don't even receive the compensation listed for my position."

"We'll check into that."

I contacted HR and sent them my requests. I didn't hear back. I followed up with my superior. Still nothing from HR. I created a proposal and presented it. I received the following message: "I am sorry, but at this time, we cannot justify a pay rate increase. Please review it again with us in six months to a year's time."

Covid had flooded the schools with cash, and they couldn't justify a pay raise. Covid itself justified a pay raise. Oh, and that part about measuring my compensation against other school districts: other than Rutherford County, no districts exist anywhere near Nashville that boast our population. It would be like comparing New York to Huetter, Idaho. Plus, I'd already brought the Rutherford County compensation schedule to the meeting.

I put the cap on the bottle, and they said, "Hmm . . . why didn't we think of that?" and walked away. They didn't need me anymore. I'd capped. I felt defeated. I felt like a nobody. I felt like I didn't matter. Nobody cared.

It sounds like I'm complaining. I am. The bottom line is that since I solved the problem, HR behaved like a problem didn't exist. They looked around and thought, *Things seem to be running smoothly around here.* Yeah. Because I made it that way.

They couldn't hear the chaos because of all the quiet I created. Maybe I should make some more noise.

Provoked to Purpose

René Descartes wrote, "Divide each difficulty into as many parts as is feasible and necessary to resolve it." That's what I did. I divided by two, me and you. I got ignored. No problem. I took the ignorance as a provocation, and it provoked me to purpose. What's my purpose? To tell my story so people will use it as a platform to burgeon themselves into becoming the person they want to be. If I'm called to stay, I'll stay, and if I'm called to go. I'll go. And if it's all so easy, just make another me.

I left.

Secret Keeper

Analyze

After reading this chapter, I feel

Shree Walker

Neverland

Peter Pan chose not to grow up. Not that he couldn't, but he didn't want to. He led a group of Lost Boys, some very lost boys, in a land of eternal infancy. Trapped in Neverland, trapped by their own choices, they remained children forever. They behaved like children, and they desired the freedom of adulthood, just not the responsibility. They never matured.

I followed Peter Pan. I had met him several years prior as a student attending John Freemont High School. He was my teacher. After high school graduation, I returned to my alma mater and worked as a teacher's assistant. During that time, I fully verified that my passion for teaching surpassed an interest or a childhood dream. I sprang some fairy wings. I had a knack. The law required that I attend college and get educated. I shouldered the responsibility, like an adult, and pursued my childhood dream. I took flight. Years later, I, like Tinker Bell, chased Peter out to the coast.

Prior to leaving my previous school district, I contacted Peter and discovered I could seek a position in Neverland. I applied, and I transferred, and I knew I left the bottle cap mentality behind. I headed back to "The Land," to Neverland, where people tackled issues as they arose. In "The Land," issues don't go unresolved. They're attacked.

Secret Keeper

Severland

I grew up in Los Angeles, south of Central Avenue, in the Jordan Downs Projects. I know the hood, and it's never too far away. I moved to Nashville as an adult child, at the age of twenty-one. Back in "The Land," my community consisted of Black and Brown, and often we ended up black and blue. That's the way it was.

When I returned to Los Angeles in my forties, things had changed. The "hood" was still the "hood," but a portal existed between Los Angeles and Watts. I landed on the other side of the portal. Somewhere between the north and the south, an unforeseen portal carried me from reality to fantasy. I learned, very quickly, I had to sever my perception of home from the reality where I landed. I landed in Neverland. Neverland, never again.

Hooked

"Hey, Peter! I never heard back from that job application."
"Hey, Peter! I got an interview for another position."
"Hey, Peter! I got a second interview."
"Hey, Peter! I got a third."
"Hey, Peter . . ."

When I arrived in Neverland, things were not as they seemed. The community housed primarily Latino and Asian families, as did the schools, but Black and Brown don't always mix. I landed the job and went to work immediately—for a lower pay rate than quoted when I applied. They like magic in Neverland. The hook sunk in. At least I'd be working with Peter. At least I'd be working with a diverse population.

After a few weeks, my internal alarm blared, *You're a grown woman on an island with boys.* I ignored it. *What difference does it make if they are men or boys? As long as I do my job, I'll be fine.* I was hooked.

Sprinkled with Fairy Dust

A concerned parent asked for a modification to a pre-K restroom. She made her request, followed the protocol, and I established a meeting. The assistant shipbuilder and I coordinated the meeting, and I brought a few of my shipmates with me. Since they'd lived in Neverland for some time and had exposure to the issues with the ships, I needed their input. Peter called.

"Hey, Peter! Glad you called me this time."

"Shree, you can't have that meeting."

"Huh?"

"You can't have Janice and Sandy in the meeting with you. The assistant shipbuilder said you wanted Janice and Sandy with you, but we *never* do that here. Not on our ships."

"Is the meeting canceled?"

"No, you meet with the assistant shipbuilder. Alone."

"Okay . . ."

They love titles in Neverland.

I ran out of the room, hustled down the hall, and informed Janice and Sandy they were disinvited. I shrugged my shoulders, like, "I don't know," hustled back, and joined the call with the assistant shipbuilder.

"So, Shree, what do you think we should do?"

"I think we should enforce the law. Give the student what he is entitled to based on his IEP. We must meet the educational needs of the student."

"Right. Hey, we're the only people on this call. What do you really think we should do?"

"I think we should do what I just said. What's the problem?"

"There's no problem. I just want to make sure you're successful."

I sneezed. *Wait! I thought I was Tinker Bell! Where'd they get this fairy dust?* The call ended.

Peter called me again. "Shree, what should we do about the situation?"

"As I said, we should uphold the student's IEP. Peter, what's the problem?"

"There's no problem. I just want to make sure you are successful. We *never* have problems, only solutions waiting to be discovered."

"Okay, Peter."

More fairy dust. Or was it sawdust?

Hook

Captain Hook ravages Neverland. Parading around like a tiger among housecats, he functions as a grown man, but he nurtures the kitten within. He's angry that he's grown, and he's angry he can't still be a little kitten and play with a ball of string. He looks like a man, but inside . . .

Peter grew up. On the exterior, he'd transformed into Captain Hook, but inside, he longed to be Peter again. Never growing up. He and his crew captured Tinker Bell and spread that fairy dust like marijuana. They promised the fairy dust made things better, but the shipmates stayed hungry and broke.

Never Jeans in Neverland

We had a solution waiting to be discovered. In our district, a no jeans policy existed in the unwritten annals of time. In our industry, jeans represent buried treasure, only available on Fridays. Yet several people wore jeans daily. My shipmates came to me asking if we could wear jeans on the ship at the end of the workweek. I asked my captain.

"There's a no jeans policy. Our ships have a no jeans policy, so we can't wear jeans. Other ships may allow jeans, but we don't allow jeans. If you want to wear jeans, it's your choice, but I wouldn't. I wouldn't wear jeans in your position."

"What do you mean in my position? Is there a problem with my position?"

"No, not in your position. There's no problem."

Let me guess. Just a solution looking to be found?

Our handbook measured the depth of six pages: a few napkins folded over, stapled together, and copied at Kinkos. No jeans policy existed. I am not sure any policy existed other than "Never behave like an adult." We had a meeting with several shipmates. One daringly ventured we call Captain Hook so he could advise on the jeans. He arrived, and we asked, "Is this a no jeans district?" Captain Hook tugged on the leg of his jeans to indicate his answer.

We *never* answered a question directly. We sent mixed messages through implication and body language. We *never* used our words to express it, not when we could stuff it in a bottle and let it float about in the ocean.

The cork popped. That's when I realized I didn't fit. I wasn't a Wendy but more like a *Jet* magazine piled in with *Reader's Digest*, or *In Living Color* thrown in with *The Golden Girls*, or Beyonce in Mayberry. I didn't . . .

Robin's Egg

A red-breasted robin will sometimes sneak into the chicken coop and lay an egg in the hen's nest. The coop appears inviting and well-fortified, but a robin's flawed thinking quickly reveals itself. A robin's blue eggs stand out in a coop full of white and brown ones.

In the fleet of ships where I sailed, Black people comprised about one percent of the population. One. As far as I knew, I represented the only Black person in the top tier of the fleet. The other one was thrown overboard months after I arrived. The few others in leadership positions functioned as first mates on their ships. Never the captain. Blue eggs get uninvited attention from the hens. They're noticed, but not nurtured. They're ignored.

We had another meeting. They love meetings in Neverland. The room grew dark. The lights dimmed, leaving only an illuminated screen and me to be seen. I presented in the dark, the lone light shining in the room. When I finished, I received an ovation. Looks of shock and inspiration beamed from the other shipmates. Seriously though, I blew that presentation out of the park! Everybody loved it. They wanted more, and they were blown away. Maybe I'd be nurtured after all.

Captain Hook walked by and shifted his one eye toward me approvingly. He hooked his phone and sent me a text message. "I am so proud of you."

From five feet away! Five feet away, and he couldn't just say, "Hey, I'm proud of you," in front of the room? No. Not with all the shipmates in there. Not in Neverland. We *never* do that. Not for blue eggs.

He tolerated me. It reminded me of *Blink* by Malcolm Gladwell, which postulates that we have this intuitive response, a rapid cognition that occurs in certain situations, that is both protective and savvy. He called it "thin-slicing." Most of us call it "a gut feeling." I thin-sliced the situation at that moment. Not the situation, but the look on Hook's face. Something sparked. He displayed admiration and disgust simultaneously. Abusers do that. They lust after and loathe their victims concurrently. I'd seen that look before. I'd seen that hook before. Passive-aggressive response. Threatened. He knew if one person addressed the issues and confronted them head-on, with eyes wide open, it would rock the boat. We *never* rocked the boat. But dang, did he want him some of that confidence—and the praise that came with it.

Time wore me thin. I had another meeting with both my immediate captain and Captain Hook, who commanded the whole fleet. My immediate captain's feelings hurt her, and she wanted me to apologize for answering a legal question with a legal answer. She pouted. He messaged me through the Zoom app and said, "Quit being so defensive." I leaned toward the screen, pressed my face close, and said, "If I seem defensive, I am." He pouted.

I didn't like being handled. I wanted to handle the situation at hand. I'd been disrespected and shoved aside too many times. I could see the ship sinking, and I worked desperately to bail out all the water. I tore the patches off the holes and replaced them with new boards. Every time I made improvements, I heard, "We *never* do that." I shined my light, but that made the ship uncomfortable. It illuminated too many holes.

Unhooked

I became unhooked. My captain, my direct supervisor, demonstrated a capacity to mishandle situations that surpassed my ability to keep sailing. Captain Hook, still somehow in charge of the entire fleet, renewed her contract for another year. The shipmates balked and stared, but nobody cared. We *never* did anything to disrupt the status quo because that meant a shift in power. And power intoxicates. One cannot see clearly who imbibes power. They cannot walk on dry land. They walk like a drunk man, on sea legs.

I decided I was finished being a secret. I knew my worth. I resigned. Tinker Bell flew the coop! Even in my resignation, chaos reigned.

"Don't tell your team. We need to wait until everything is processed with the shipmasters who protect the ship."

"Okay, but don't we need a succession plan?"

"Sure. We are working on that."

Two weeks passed, and I had another conversation with Captain Hook.

"Hey, Captain Hook. I heard from my shipmates today that you told them I'd be departing the ship. Is that true?"

"They know you'll be leaving the ship, and we are diligently searching for a replacement captain. Don't you worry."

"What about my resignation? I need to let the whole fleet know I am resigning. Several people still need training, and they will need to know whom to contact after I depart."

"Hold off on that. We'll let you know when to notify everyone."

That day never came. I took the liberty to send my own message, not in a bottle, to all the shipmates in the fleet. A mass email. We *never* do that, not without permission.

We had a final meeting, and when the meeting ended, nobody mentioned my departure. I took it upon myself to take the floor.

"For those of you who don't know, today will be my last meeting with this fleet. I appreciate all of my time and opportunity with this fleet."

Nothing.

I couldn't be a secret any longer. I had a purpose. I had been provoked to purpose.

I launched a speaking career, and it has become wildly successful—beyond my expectations. I don't hide behind the secrets anymore. The secrets trapped me and stole my value. I don't need to be noticed either; it doesn't matter. The message matters. As long as I deliver the message. My purpose is to tell my story. To tell my story so we all know our secrets don't make us special; they clip our wings and attach us to strings.

Tinker Bell flies with no strings attached. Yet one problem is she can't speak. Not like we do. Her voice makes the tinkling sound of, well, a tinker. She can't speak, but when she sprinkles her fairy dust, the game changes and people start flying. Unlike the sawdust Peter and the assistant shipbuilder used, Tinker Bell's fairy dust makes sure she is *heard.*

That is a portion of my purpose—to eradicate voicelessness. Being voiceless doesn't mean a person cannot speak. Rather, they can't be heard.

Tink helps people be heard, so they can resolve their issues, their past. Not hide from it or pretend it doesn't exist.

People need to be reunited, not ignored, so I fly with purpose. My purpose is to place myself underneath his purpose. To be a voice for the voiceless, and to teach the voiceless to be heard.

But what about my lists?

Shree Walker

Evaluate

Before reading this chapter, I thought

After reading this chapter, I now think

The List

My hand scrawled across the page. The ever-flowing words eloquently raced through the air into my ears. My page moved rapidly under the quick movements of my hand, racing to write it all out. Our history professor's voice increased in intensity. Students sighed, filling the room with anxious breaths. A chair squeaked. One stood. She struggled forward, down the aisle, toward the exit.

She stopped. Next to my elbow, she peered over my shoulder. I waited. Something heinous was in the air. I looked up and met her eyes. "My, you got a long grocery list."

"Yes, I do."

She didn't know. She didn't know I had a long laundry list. Shame-faced, I turned my eyes back to the page. *I've got to stop. This is crazy. I'll never escape this way.*

Escape

I escaped the trauma of my past when I boarded that plane flying from Los Angeles to Nashville. At twenty-one years old, I thought changing environments would change me. I was naive.

Shree Walker

When the plane descended through the clouds and I saw the trees near the ground, I knew I'd found my new home. Away from the abuse, away from the noise, away from my past. I'd be one with nature, one with Nashville. What I didn't know was that my past would follow me, chase me, and the monsters would accompany me.

I met wonderful people at Fisk University, and I very much enjoyed my time there. But there's a dark side few know about.

Nashville radiated vitality, and although Fisk is a Historically Black College and University, I ended up surrounded by white folk. White country folk who populated 2nd Avenue, Broadway, and West End. In Los Angeles, I experienced many traumatic experiences: sexual abuse at home, sexual abuse at the hand of a friend, inappropriate touching by my grandfather, men exposing themselves to me, and rape. In Nashville, I experienced welcoming calls, banjo music, line dancing, and inclusion, even among the white folk. (I say this all tongue-in-cheek).

I brought some baggage with me from Los Angeles—a shadow army of survival skills: seduction and disassociation. While in Nashville, I worked my ass off. I attended school during the day and worked at Blockbuster and H.H. Gregg and Best Buy at night. I often had three jobs at a time. I had learned to hustle in Los Angeles as well as some other things too. My childhood taught me to question myself, *What's wrong with me?* My adulthood taught me to use my superpowers. I arrived at Fisk old enough to buy alcohol, a badass Black woman with a bangin' body.

And I paid my way through school.

All Work for No Pay

"Hey, Shree, you working tonight?"
"Yeah, Ronnie. Blockbuster's tonight."
"You know Jamal wants to holler at you, don't you?"
"Then why don't he holler?"
"I don't know. I guess he heard you still messin' with No Name down there in Texas."
"I ain't messin' with No Name. He's my boyfriend, but what's that got to do with Jamal?"
"You know what he call you?"

"What?"

"Shree with the tattoo."

"That's stupid. Like I'm the only girl around here with a tattoo."

"No, you the only grown woman around here with a tattoo. He want to be with you because you about your business. If he can break that, another set of panties on the wall."

"I'm a trophy."

"Yup."

"Ronnie. You know little boys be stupid."

"Yup. So is little girls."

He was right. I was about my business. I needed to finish school so I could move on with my life. Success stretched out like a one-way street, no turning back, and I felt like I had gotten a late start. What was I doing, a grown woman, messing around with little boys? And those jobs were killing me. Working eight hours for sixty or seventy dollars? I wanted something new.

Body or Brains

I liked to connect on a soul level. I enjoyed intellectual pursuits and philosophical conversations, delving deep into the mysteries of life to figure out what made people tick. My body often betrayed me. Men pursued what I could offer, not what I brought to the table. Other men—older men—searched my eyes and perceived an old soul looking to unite with a like mind. We held each other transfixed, suspended, until the night ended.

Broadway runs deep into the heart of Nashville. Somewhere in the abdomen, Broadway transforms into West End Avenue. Broadway runs downtown, while West End runs uptown. One follows Broadway to the party and West End to the money. I'd been to the party. I wanted the money.

One night, dressed to the nine's, I walked past the line outside Ruth's Chris Steakhouse. A whisper.

"Gorgeous moon out tonight, isn't it?"

"Say what?"

"The moon. It's gorgeous, isn't it?"

"Men have been using comments about the moon to pick up women for millennia. It's not going to work."

"No, men have aspired to reach heavenly bodies for millennia. The moon represents something out of reach, a golden goose egg by which a man can measure his prowess. But men are fools because the heavenly bodies truly exist here on earth."

"Who said that? Pascal?"

"Maybe Flaubert."

"What about the moon?"

"Would you like to have a drink with me tonight under the moon?"

"Sure, I would like that."

We entered the steakhouse and were escorted to a table. We shared drinks and dinner and white tablecloth service. Our conversation centered mostly on how people are often a murky representation of their true selves. How fear and culture bind people into conformity, all while their souls long for free expression. I saw the direction the night was moving. Although I enjoyed his company, and the expensive dinner flattered me, I had different intentions.

"John, you're nice to talk to, but I need you to know that I don't do one-night stands."

"Good. How about six nights?"

"What?"

"How about six nights?"

"I don't know. How are we going to do that?"

He ran his fingers through his salt-and-pepper hair, his Cartier watch gleaming. He smiled. The skin around his eyes creased ever so slightly into crow's feet. His teeth showed small tobacco stains from years of smoking cigars.

"You don't worry about that. I will take care of it. I'll tell you which restaurant, and I'll take care of the hotel. I pay $450 for the evening and $700 for the night."

"You're kind of forward, aren't you?"

"I'm a businessman. This is business."

He adjusted his glasses.

"I'm not into that."

A slight frown, followed by a twinkle in his eye. A look, like there was something he needed to conquer.

"You're not into sharing an evening with a man, being wined and dined, stimulated with deep conversation, and paid for it? Sounds like something most women would do for free. Or are you not into me calling it a business transaction?"

"Where's the dang hotel?"

"Follow me to my car."

Around four in the morning, I told him I needed to go. He kicked his black-and-white wingtips out of his way and walked to the restroom. I spoke through the closed door.

"John, my roommates will be worried. I have to leave soon."

"The money's on the dresser. Pick it up on your way out."

"John! This is $900! You said $450."

He walked out of the restroom.

"I'm a big tipper."

"You know I don't do this, right? For a living."

"Then why were you walking down West End alone at night, dressed to kill?"

My Body, Your Blessing

Then why were you walking down West End alone at night, dressed to kill? Then why were you walking down West End alone at night, dressed to kill?

His question haunted me. Was this my intention? Did I subconsciously choose this life before I consciously chose to participate? I know I wasn't walking down the street selling my body. I wasn't an escort service. He misunderstood; however, when he presented the opportunity, it seemed more possible, more like, *If I'm eventually going to give up my body, why not get paid while doing it? I'll take a few thousand to perform and disappear.* I wondered if I were deceiving myself, like a person who says, "I may snort cocaine, but I won't do crack," or "I may go to the strip club, but I won't pay for sex."

Women seem to have an innate desire to sacrifice their bodies for others. Women carry children in their wombs and sacrifice their breasts to feed them. Women scrape their fingers to the bone to clean a house, cook a meal, or run a machine in a machine shop. Women undergo countless surgeries to satisfy a man who'll never be satisfied with one woman.

My body, my choice? More like my body, their benefit. I added John's name to the list. And that's how it was. I attended school during the morning, worked my jobs in the evenings, and worked the street on the weekends. Now I didn't work the street in the traditional sense. I met distinguished men, in distinguished places, for distinguished evenings. And then they would pay me. Sometimes for the evening. Sometimes to go away.

Back at Fisk, I had male friends who didn't have money. I saw their refrigerators filled with bottled water and some old takeout, and I'd take them to the store.

"Ronnie, you still ain't got not groceries?"

"No, Re. I don't get paid until Friday."

"Let's go get some groceries."

"Shree, I don't have no money."

"I'm buyin'."

"Where you get all this money? I know Blockbuster ain't payin' all that much."

"I told you when I came here. I had money from working back home. Don't worry about it. Let's go get some groceries."

I felt like a body actress. My body got me into the movie, and if I showed it, I got paid more, but I'd never have a speaking part. Just a part where a man had meaningless sex with me to titillate the viewers, but when the credits rolled, nobody looked for "Naked Girl at the Beginning." But to me, the sex wasn't meaningless; it just wasn't whole.

My body paid for my school. My body paid for my bills. My body paid for my friends who couldn't pay for themselves. My body paid for an end. I wanted a real relationship, to be fully known, but I wielded the only superpowers I knew: seduction and disassociation.

Seduction brought in the men. We didn't always have sex. Many times, we had dinner and meaningful conversations. Other times, sex. With or without, I got paid.

Disassociation pushed the men away. During a sexual experience, all that mattered was what happened in my head. I played the story I chose, and I connected with that story, not the experience. Often, I did not register the experience, even a climax, because I performed for the story in my mind. I served them to serve me.

And I added names to my list.

Building the List

"Something inside me snapped!"

"What are you talking about."

"When I moved here, something inside me snapped. I was still in a relationship with No Name, but I was angry. Angry at the world. Angry at him. Angry at myself."

"Okay, but didn't you say he was cheatin' on you?"

"Sure, but I'm no angel, Ronnie. I have my scars. I have my scars."

"Don't we all?"

"You know where I get my money?"

"Strippin'! Just kidding."

"About the same."

"Hookin'? Nah. Re, I don't believe that."

"It ain't like that. Sometimes I get paid to date."

"What was all that 'something inside me snapped' stuff? If you workin' to get paid, you workin' to get paid."

"I'm workin' to get even."

"With who?"

"Me, I guess. I don't know. But it ain't workin'. I'm not happy. I'm angry. Sometimes I think that bastard ruined my life."

"Who's that?"

"Nobody."

And I built the list. Name after name after name. I can list the name of every sexual partner I had in order. In freakin' order. Something broke inside me somewhere, and I searched for meaning through connection, through sex. I didn't find it. All I found was a list.

Burning the List

"My, you got a long grocery list!"

Yeah, I do. But that's not the crazy part. The crazy part is I carried the list around with me.

When I looked away, shamefaced, a junior in college, with a very, very long list of lovers, I asked myself, *What are you carrying this around for?*

I never got a good answer. I decided to be more discreet with my body. Still, at night, I'd slink out to West End. Still, I'd play games in my mind, theater.

"You wish I were your wife and not her, right?"

"Every day."

"Why not leave her?"

"Money."

"But you love me, right?"

"Forget the money. I'll choose you."

But that never happened. I burned the list. Making the list brought the light into my eyes, just like when an alcoholic makes a spiritual inventory during their fourth step. After making my inventory, I confessed it, and I asked God for help. I made amends with myself. I decided to reduce my partners. If I slept with one last month, then I'd sleep with none for the next two months. The weight had grown to be too much to bear, so I made my list, learned from it, then burned it.

Secret Keeper

Create

After reading this chapter, I will restore myself by

Shree Walker

Number Two

Every list begins with *A*. A mistake. My first consensual sexual experience occurred at the age of sixteen. Prior to that, all sexual experiences fell into the category of abuse and predatory. My monster, my neighbor, my grandfather. Then, at sixteen, I told Momma, "I'm gonna have sex with my boyfriend," while she pretended to sleep on the couch. Thanatosis. Toxic immobility. Playing dead. Playing possum. It's a pretty good indicator of previous abuse.

I built my list from that one stupid mistake. That one stupid choice. But the second one haunts me even more.

Teacher's Pet

How can I answer the question "Who was your favorite teacher?" I had scores of instrumental teachers. Ms. Everton. Mr. Thompson. Mrs. Jackson. I loved teachers. I didn't love school, but I loved teachers. I even spent time at Mr. Thompson's and Ms. Everton's homes. In times of crisis, my teachers often delivered me from the worst pain. I'd give anything to be a teacher.

But I wasn't stupid. That didn't mean explicit touching. I loved teachers, but I trusted *nobody*. My sixth-grade teacher, Mr. Dodson, walked down the aisle as the bell sounded. The one in my mind. Grouped in pods of four, our desks were separated by a narrow aisle. One ran directly behind me. Although I respected Mr. Dodson, nothing mattered when harm came my way.

He needed access to his desk. He walked toward me. He turned to the side and sucked in his belly. I imagined his crotch rubbing against my back, against my neck, touching my hair. I hit the deck. I dove onto the floor and knocked two chairs out of the way. Shay, sitting across from me, jumped and screeched. Mr. Dodson helped me up and said, "What's wrong, Shree?"

I told the truth this time. "I thought . . . I thought you were going to touch me." Mr. Dodson behaved cautiously and respectfully around me after that day. He truly was a great teacher and very helpful. I think he knew I had some trauma, so he intentionally decreased the opportunity for misbehavior in our class. Unlike some other teachers in my future, Mr. Dodson built my trust and never broke it.

Teachers Pet

As I began Freemont High School, I searched for belonging. I joined the dance team, became a manager for the football team, ran track, played softball, and got a boyfriend. I'd already had an odd relationship with the sports medicine manager, but it wasn't romantic or sexual. He just gave me too much liberty and too much information. Eventually, he was prosecuted for possession.

One day, while I was fooling around in the gym with a basketball, a young, white male teacher walked in: Mr. Baylor. He coached softball and basketball.

"Hey, do you play?"

"No, Coach."

"You look like a capable athlete. What sports do you play?"

"This year, I wanna play softball. I run track, and I'll do drill team or cadets or something."

"Do you want to try out for basketball?"

"No. I'll save it, but I'll see you during softball season."

"Sounds good."

That ended our meeting. An innocuous conversation in the gym about sports. The year progressed. I saw Mr. Baylor more and more. I never got any odd vibes from him, and I was attuned to vibes. Typically, I could identify a character of violence in mere seconds. Mr. Baylor seemed like a young grandpa, full of concern and wisdom, but with high energy. Who knew that he petted?

Into the Fire

One day several months later, after our softball tournament, several girls rode back to Mr. Baylor's house, located a hundred yards from the beach. He lived on Manhattan Beach and invited us over all the time. Our parents knew about it and picked us up from his house one by one. Bye, Gracie. Bye, Janet. Bye, Shay. By myself.

Help! I never thought I'd be by myself in his home. Well, no big deal. Mr. Baylor was cool and had been the coach of the girls' basketball and softball teams for years. He sat on his couch reading.

"Shree, have you ever read *Of Mice and Men*?"

"No."

"What about *The Crucible*?"

"No. What's that about?"

He made a space for me on the couch. I decided I could trust him. He had to take me home later, so he wouldn't try anything. And he loved talking, literature, sports, and his students. I sat down.

"It's about this girl, Abigail, wielding her power in a Puritan colony in the 1600s. See, John Proctor, a successful farmer in his mid-thirties, had an affair with her. And she used that information to blackmail him."

Someone, please help.

"She knew if he told, he'd be excommunicated, so she dangled the lust over his head."

"What did he do?"

I scooted away.

"It's not important what he did. It's important what she did. At seventeen years old, she held the village of Salem—and John Proctor, for that matter—in her hand."

"Cool."

Secret Keeper

"You have that power too, Shree. You just need to learn to harness it."

His hand touched my thigh. *Please help!* All the way up. Naturally, I had to get out of there. Now his hand rubbed my breasts. Then he kissed me. First, my shoulder, then my neck, then my mouth. *Why are men so dirty, with their dirty, dirty hands?*

"Mr. Baylor? I have to go to the restroom right now!" I jumped up, hustled through the kitchen, and locked myself in the restroom. I couldn't call Momma, or anyone for that matter, but I could wait until he calmed down, until he got the picture. Twenty minutes passed.

"Shree, are you all right in there?"

"Yes, Mr. Baylor. I'll be right out. Sorry, my stomach is upset." *Good one. Nobody wants a girl with diarrhea.* I waited about ten more minutes and slowly opened the bathroom door.

I snuck out of the bathroom, into the kitchen, and looked in his den. He sat on the couch, staring out the window as if nothing had happened. I made a noise in the kitchen, grabbed a glass, filled it with water, and walked around the corner.

"Mr. Baylor, I'm ready to go home now."

He sat on the couch with his penis in his hand and looked up at me. "You want to be Abigail, and I'll be Proctor?"

"Mr. Baylor, I'm ready to go home now. I'm sick."

Payoff

He drove me home in silence, looking straight through the bug-covered windshield. I looked at him one time, turned, and faced out my window. *Abigail. What the hell is wrong with white people? Only they would fantasize about a Puritan.* When we pulled up, he put the car in park and didn't say a word to me.

Momma came walking out to the car, and Mr. Baylor got out and greeted her.

"Hello, Ms. Walker. How are you?"

"Just fine. Thank you for taking care of my Shree here."

"Oh, no problem. She played well in the tournament, and the girls had fun at the beach afterward. She's a great kid. Glad to have her. You're a lucky mom. She seems a bit queasy today, not sure what's wrong. She said her stomach was upset, so we came straight home."

I rolled my eyes. Momma didn't notice. I didn't care. I'd escaped. I wouldn't make that mistake again.

"Ms. Walker. Don't worry about the dues. I'll take care of the fifty dollars."

"Oh! Thank you, Mr. Baylor! You're so sweet."

"No problem. Bye, Shree. We'll see you on Monday."

"Bye, Coach."

Fifty dollars? Abigail would have charged more than that. I should have gone Lorena Bobbitt on him. As James Baldwin said, "Children have never been very good at listening to their elders, but they have never failed to imitate them."[2] I did what I knew. I did what I saw other women do, what I learned in the projects, what everybody did. I kept my mouth shut.

Paid to Go Away

Before vision boards were registered as an activity, I built collages. I collected materials from my favorite magazines and built collages on corkboards to express a message. Sometimes the message spoke to me, other times to the world.

Mr. Baylor owned several *J. Crew* magazines. I'd never been exposed to their clothes, and I loved the magazine. I adored this one skirt in his November catalog. Black and white, the skirt appeared to move when the girl did, like an extension of her body, full of grace and class. For years, I'd worn clothes too large for me, attempting to cover my body. The day Baylor molested me, I had on this old bra, all raggedy and worn, but it was my favorite. Now I hated it.

I loved that skirt. I'd grown accustomed to wearing large clothes, then I changed my style, but after Baylor exposed himself, I went back to large, too large. I still put that skirt on my corkboard. Near the end of the school year, he walked by and threw a plastic bag on my desk. I opened it. He'd bought the skirt for me. He'd gone through the magazine, found the

---

[2] James Baldwin, *Nobody Knows My Name* (New York: Vintage Books, 1993), 61.

missing piece, got another copy of the magazine to compare, located the skirt, and gone to J. Crew and bought it for me.

Just like the older white men in my future, he paid me to go away. This time, it disgusted me. I didn't know that one day in the future, I'd volunteer for relationships that paid me to go away. Mr. Baylor made the list. Number 2. I never slept with him, but he and his number 2 pencil made the list. Because he broke me. He broke me because he convinced me that the problem was me. I knew the people in my past had problems, but he was a teacher. And if a teacher wanted to pet me, then something must be wrong with me.

Years later, Mr. Baylor married one of his students. It wasn't me. Something was wrong with him. According to Arthur Miller, John Proctor's list began with *A*, and John Proctor, well, he was hanged while Abigail escaped. Look it up. Read what folklore said happened to her. Hidden men and their hidden lives create hideous history.

Shree Walker

Apply

Because of my experience reading this chapter, now I will

Mo Problems

In the late 1990s, Puff Daddy (now P. Diddy), Biggie, and Mase collaborated on the song "Mo Money, Mo Problems." During Biggie's solo—shout-out to my East Coast friends—he asked where all the players were. He wanted them to out themselves. I can answer his question. I can tell him where all the players were.

All over. They don't want to be identified. Instead, they hide. They play games. That's why they're called *players*.

Mo Meaningful

I ran through Percy Warner Park, completing a five-mile loop. Exhilarated by the rustling leaves, bustling squirrels, and my own heart, I circled around the home stretch. Shrouded in mystery, a black mass huddled near the side of the trail as the sun crept through the trees. A man stood quickly, whirled around, and stepped into my path.

"Oh! Pardon me. I did not mean to disturb you!"

"Well, when you jump out at somebody like that—"

"I know. I know. My most sincere apologies. I'm sure it was rather disturbing seeing a man lurch from a posture of reverence."

"Yes. Jumping out at me early in the morning scared me. Bye."

"No. I'm sorry. Let me make it up to you."
"I have this run to finish, and then I have to get to work."
"Where do you work?"
"Man, I don't give random people my whereabouts."
"I'm not random. This was orchestrated by God."
"What?"
"Blessed be his name."
"I don't follow."
"I prayed for wisdom and insight, and I turn, and there you are."
"You think I'm an answer to prayer?"
"Who am I to argue?"
"I don't know. Who are you?"
"Mo. You can call me Mo. I am a seeker of wisdom."
"Did you find it?"
"I found you."
"Cute."
"Magnificent. Likewise, for what are you searching?"
"Meaning."
"Isn't the meaning of life to serve God in our flesh?"
"I need to finish my run."
"You run to feel free. I feel free enough to run. We are different. I will walk with you on your path."
"No. I'll walk alone."
"I will walk with you to keep you safe. It is my duty."
"Do you always speak so formally? We're not at church, you know."
"I don't attend church."
"But you pray?"
"Yes. I pray daily. I pray for wisdom, and I pray for peace. Do you pray?"
"I pray. I pray for my students."
"Oh, you are a teacher. Teaching the blind to see?"
"Something like that."

He escorted me to my car "to ensure I arrived safely." We continued speaking for a few minutes, and I nearly forgot the interaction—an odd conversation with an odd yet interesting man.

I ran into him again a few weeks later. At a different time, but at the same park. We had a meaningful conversation. A sharply handsome man, he asked for my number. I asked him, "You got a girlfriend?"
"No."
"A wife?"
"No."
"You single?"
"Yes."
"You sure?"
"Yes."
"Here's my number." I had reservations, but how dangerous could he be? I woke up early to run; he woke up early to pray. Who was I to judge?

He should have said, "I *prey*."

Mo Religion

"We, too, believe Jesus descended from God and is now seated at his right hand. We believe Jesus came to lead us to God."
"But you don't believe he is God's Son?"
"How can God have a Son?"
"I don't know."
"We are not that different, you and I; I just believe the Prophet brought more revelation, the final revelation, but we don't discount the message of Jesus. We honor it."
"Do you believe a man can have multiple wives?"
"Oh, some believe that. I don't practice that. I believe a man may have four wives, but *Islam* means peace, and how can you have peace with four wives in the same house?"
"Cute."
"No. Magnificent."
"Mo, you make me laugh. What about four wives in four separate houses?"
"Mo wives, less peace. No wives, Mo peace."
"Good one."
The Three Stooges had a character named Moe. He was a schmuck.

Shree Walker

Mo Time

Mo and I spent more and more time together. Our conversations spanned religion, race, cultural identity, politics, the rights of women, and pretty much everything. The conversations increased in depth, as did our relationship. We did not have sex. I'd learned that lesson too many times; no more names on the list. Mo often came to my apartment. We'd meet for dinner or lunch, but he restricted his diet, so we often just met at my place. One time, he even bought me a cake for my birthday, but he "eschewed cake, for cake contains gelatin, and we cannot eat gelatin."

I respected him. He never touched me. Sure, he made advances, like any man, but he never forced the issue. Never forced the issue. I'd had many relationships with many men that were not sexual whatsoever in nature, but with Mo, it was different. He was different. We connected on a deep level, and even as a single man, he never tried to touch me. I respected him. No, Mo. No Mo respect.

Mo Sex

We had sex. It was awful. When I say awful, I mean soul-depriving and heart-wrenching. I didn't connect. No movie played in my head. I had no story to tell. I didn't want to do it in the first place. I felt like I had blasphemed myself and ruined a true connection. He felt different. He didn't understand. Mo was a gentleman, though. He never pushed the issue of more sex.

No Mo Sex

"No, Mo. We can't have sex again. It doesn't feel right. I don't mean you don't feel right. I mean it doesn't feel right. Something in my spirit tells me it's wrong."

"You should listen to your spirit. I believe our spirits can communicate things our minds cannot conceive. I also believe that a man and a woman unite their souls when they have a sexual union. You and I have a sexual union, a spiritual one. I am not offended. When the time is right, you will know."

Oh no.

Mo continued. "You mentioned you are struggling to pay for your tuition?"

"Yes. Now I am. Once I pay this month, I'll be good."

"You may borrow the money from me and pay it back."

"Mo! I can't do that. I'd never do that!"

I did that. I borrowed the money and paid him back. We continued our relationship, and we maintained a non-physical one. I believed him. Our spirits united as time elapsed, and we understood each other. I considered it. What would it be like to be his wife? Would the sexual encounters change when we got married? He clearly loved me, protected me, and cared for me deeply. I cared for him. Oh, Mo!

Mo Fear

Mo descended the stairs in a rush. He had to go. He was running late, so after a quick embrace, he ran down the stairs. He forgot his watch. I raced down after him. We raced back up. Something spooked him.

"They are Kurdish. I cannot go down there. They know me."

"What the hell's the problem? You can't walk out of an apartment and get in your car? What's the problem?"

"I know them. We worship together. I cannot allow them to see me."

"See you or see me?"

"See me."

Yeah, right. I knew what had happened. His fear-panicked face told the lie his lips denied. Down on his knees to pray? No. Down on his knees to prey. He was devout, all right, devoutly devoted to himself. He didn't want them to know about me.

My cheeks burned. I paced around the apartment and peeked out the window. *Why am I peeking out of my window? What did I do wrong?* Nothing. I asked him to leave.

Dirty men with dirty hands make me feel dirty. Mo made me feel dirty with his fear. Like I was dirty. Like I brought shame on his head. He couldn't be seen with me outside my apartment? No Mo, no more.

Shree Walker

No Mo, No More

Mo disappeared like a faithless prayer. He vaporized after one step too close to being caught with an infidel. Love lost meaning that day. I found myself in my bathroom, hunched over the sink, looking full-faced into the mirror as streams poured from my eyes, my mouth wide open, wishing I'd vomit. But it wouldn't come out. That pain that raged in my stomach churned around reluctantly, doubling me over my vanity, and resided.

I cried out to God. "Why? Why? Why? Why didn't you answer my prayers? I tried to stay pure this time. I loved him. I wanted a family. Why? Why? Why?"

He didn't answer. I supposed he didn't care. Too many men. Too many bad experiences. I broke back into my routines. No Mo, no more. The days seemed short, and the nights seemed long. My friendships resumed full force. Like I had vanished, I reemerged back on the scene. Back to hanging out with friends, listening to live music, doing life. God, I missed it. I never realized I'd hidden myself away with Mo.

Why?

Mo Family

The midmorning sun crested the trees. I ran through Percy Warner Park, completing a five-mile run. Exhilarated by the rustling leaves, bustling squirrels, and my own heart, I circled around the home stretch. I raced down the home stretch, leaving sweat and concern in my wake. Years had passed since Mo, and I'd moved on. I never thought about him anymore—until that morning. I saw him. No Mo shrouded mystery.

I walked to my car, and a green minivan was parked next to it. Big enough to hold children. Three children, to be exact. Three children rolled out of the sides of that van, and one very-covered wife exited the passenger seat. She rode shotgun. I bet he wished he had one when he saw me.

Because he was freakin' married! That fool was married the whole time. God did care. Foolish men cheat on their wives. Players keep secrets. Foolish players return to the same playground with their wives.

Mo stepped out of the van. For all the speeches and wisdom he lavished from his tongue previously, he sure seemed tongue-tied. He looked

Secret Keeper

at me, and shame blossomed inside him, ran up his spine, and showed on his downturned face like fire. I loved it. Every moment of it.

I walked over and said hello. Head down, he greeted me half-heartedly and walked to his wife, linking his arm in hers. She saw me, She saw me, and I believe she knew. What could she say? He'd prayed for wisdom and peace, and a piece cost him both in that moment.

Maybe that was his answer. Keep your dirty hands and dirty heart off other women when you've got a family. All those "wives" and no peace.

Tupac is rumored to have said, "Everybody's at war with different things. . . . I'm at war with my own heart sometimes. At least Tupac told the truth. He knew all along the west side was the best. Maybe I shouldn't be so hard on Mo. Maybe Mo thought he and his wife were on a break.

Shree Walker

Understand

My experience reading this chapter was

Break

In education, we often build brain breaks into our lessons. Students' interest wanes quickly, and the continual flood of information sends them reeling. Their eyes gloss over, heads drop, bodies slouch. Body language aside, too much information, emotion, and energy exhumed in one setting will beat anyone down.

A brain break is not a brain brake. We create an activity that engages the brain, often the mind-body connection, and stretch out that neuroplasticity. I call it "breaking the monotony." Let's break the monotony.

Monster Break

Four thought monsters swirl around the room, circling in on us. Our task is to defeat them. If we identify them, we can replace them. Thought monsters swirl in secrets and hate to be captured. At least, that's what they want me to think. They will resist. They will fight back. They are monsters, after all.

The first thought monster is Fear, but his name is Mr. Pain. The second is the trust monster. Her name is Doubt. The third monster is a woman, always a woman. She's the inadequacy monster, and her name is

Perfectionism. The final monster is the unworthy monster. He goes by Loneliness.

The first part of our game is identification. I provide the scenario and you identify the monster.

Ready?

Let the Games Begin

Naomi moves across the dance floor swiftly. Her sparkly, silver dress moves with her, passionately. A slim girl, twenty-something, Naomi glances seductively at her boyfriend across the room, who's seated in his chair. She stares. She moves. She dances his way, clearly the object of his desire. And she's clearly the object of desire for many men in the room. Her boyfriend looks up and then back down at his feet. She keeps coming. She dances in front of him, and their eyes lock. His feet remain planted on the floor. His butt in the chair.

"Jason, let's dance. C'mon, boy. It's fun. Get out here, and you'll see."

"No, Mee Mee. I can't. Sorry. You keep dancing. You look great."

"Jason, please? I want to dance with you."

"I can't. I'm sorry."

"Jason."

He looks away. The thought monsters invaded.

Jason's thought monster is _____.

Naomi bats her eyes; her silver mascara shimmers, catching the light. Her earrings sparkle. "Jason, you play ball all day with your friends, but you can't dance with me?"

Naomi's thought monster is _____.

"Sorry, baby. I just can't."

Her tone changes. "Okay, in a minute?"

"Yeah, I promise. In a minute."

She dances away as eyes follow her lustfully. Jason doesn't notice. A new thought monster appears for Naomi. She feels _____.

Her pace slows. She crosses her arms. Jason doesn't budge, but a new thought monster emerges for him too. He feels _____.

I identified the thought monsters Perfectionism, Perfectionism, Loneliness, and Loneliness. What did you get? Did you get different answers?

How do you feel? Unworthy? Inadequate? Do you feel Fear? Doubt? Happy? Smart? Wise? Concerned? Apathetic? Bored?

Let's try another one. Monica and Kelly are at the same club. Monica's one with her body, a shorter, Black woman with several curves—too many. She's big, but she doesn't mind. Her friend Kelly, on the other hand, stands tall, thin, blonde, beautiful. Like a model. Like a Barbie.

Kelly sits in her chair, smiling, but disengaged. She catches plenty of stares but no approaches. Monica, on the other hand, is approached repeatedly. Several men dance with her. Her bright smile and bubbly laugh keep them coming in waves. She moves from man to man to man. Never staying with the same man long enough to finish more than one song. Monica's thought monster is _____.

After watching Monica dance for long enough, Kelly rises from her chair and cautiously makes her way to the floor. Her thought monster attacks. She sits back down. Kelly's thought monster is _____.

Naomi spots Monica. They share a look. Naomi dances over. Together, they dance to three songs. The night wears on. Jason spots Kelly sitting alone. He walks over, pulls up a chair, sits down, and asks if she wants a drink. She accepts. Monica catches sight of this and dances closer to Naomi, and Naomi sees it too. She presses in against Monica.

Naomi looks at Jason, and her new thought monster _____ quickly turns into _____. She presses closer to Monica.

What thought monsters did you identify? Does it really matter? Don't the thought monsters conglomerate and amalgamate into one, seamlessly interweaving in and out of each other? Does it matter? As a perfectionist, all this matters desperately. Did you feel any thought monsters creeping in, watching over you, playing with your mind?

For the record, I identified the thought monsters Doubt, Mr. Pain, Doubt, and Mr. Pain.

Identification and Multiplication

Inside my mind, the thought monsters multiply, looking for crevices in which to breed. Driving out hope, joy, confidence, and contentment, they spawn like flames, seeking branches, leaves, anything they can burn and consume. Unlike flames, the thought monsters have intellect. The thought monsters are intelligent enemies.

Thought monsters use strategy. Their first strategy is false confidence. When I know my enemy, I can defeat him. Of course, that's a *lie*. I've known many enemies I couldn't defeat, not on my own. I'd have to recruit an army, and thought monsters run in an army. Thought monsters disguise themselves as puppies: cute, cuddly, sweet. Another analogy would be lambs. I nurture them and feed them. I raise them into wolves. And they attack, and I believe I can kill them by knowing their names. But a pack of wolves is way too smart for that.

I implied their second strategy in the previous paragraph. Thought monsters use disguises. Disguised as protection, intuition, confidence, and humility, they attack. If someone offends me, I defend. Am I not righteous in my defense? Then I waver. Then I doubt. They act like friends. Insidious.

Attrition is the third strategy of the thought monsters. They don't need to win the war; they don't need to win the battle. They only need to break me down, one chunk at a time. Slowly breaking my defenses, they leave for an opportune time. This gives me time to build a defense. Not a worry for them: the little ones sneak around inside looking for breeding grounds. I'll break eventually, and they know it.

Divide and Conquer

Momma always grocery shopped on Saturdays. Goodbye Saturday morning cartoons, hello nasty supermarket. Most times, I didn't mind, especially as I aged. We'd pile into the station wagon, fighting over who got the front seat. I'd create a list of candies to buy myself in case the opportunity arose. I enjoyed shopping, navigating the prices, searching for the best deals. The responsibility made me feel grown up. In fact, Momma started sending me to the grocery store when I was eleven years old, and I returned with a full basket and a tallied total of the cost. Always under budget.

A few years later, Momma took four of us to the grocery store, and we divided and conquered. She handed each of us a handwritten list—in her artistic way—and we scoured the store for the products and the deals. The smell of Pink Oil and Blue Magic momentarily lured me to the ethnic hair aisle, as did the orange Reese's wrappers in the candy aisle. We raced in and raced out—as much as children can race through the temptations of the grocery store. This made our Saturday morning trips quicker, which rewarded everybody. Momma made the lists, we returned to Momma, and Momma took us home, usually with a treat.

Sometimes Momma became lax. She didn't notice if I snuck extra items into the cart. As long as we came in under budget—and I bagged the groceries—nobody got hurt. I wanted items not on *the* list but on *my* list. What was my thought monster? _____. We minions pilfered unlisted items to meet our undesirable demands. But who told us we couldn't have the filthy lucre?

I discovered, when battling the thought monsters, that dividing and conquering helped. When I cornered inadequacy and focused on gathering evidence of my worth, I made progress. Conversely, when I attempted to tackle my issues simultaneously, I usually got gangbanged.

When I met Leon, that was one of the issues. I'd worked so hard on tackling multiple issues that I had recovery fatigue. And during recovery fatigue, I relapsed. I would identify my issues and run full force into battling them all—and make great progress. Enough to think I'd grown safe. As a result, I became lax.

Now I know identifying and attacking my enemies is not enough, but dividing them and tackling one issue at a time sure helps. I am acutely aware that while I focus on one issue, the other thought monsters romp and play and brag about bringing back their buddies I didn't even have on the list. Little brats.

One more thought about a divide and conquer approach: focusing on one issue is attainable, but focusing on all the issues is annoying. Nothing is more annoying than listening to someone exhaustively list all their issues.

For instance, "Hi, I'm Bob, and I'm an alcoholic who struggles with codependency, narcissism, obsessive-compulsive disorder, sexual addiction, drug dependency, thoughts of self-harm, general irritability, congenital resting mad face, anger issues, pride, lust, greed, gluttony, and genital warts."

"Hi, Bob!"

Shree Walker

"Hi, I'm Shree, and I'm recovering from childhood abuse and trauma, and I struggle with people who list their issues like they're all addictions. Sorry, compulsively plucking your nose hair does not qualify as an addiction. Leave that at home.

So, for me, dividing and conquering helps. But it's not foolproof. If it were, this memoir wouldn't exist.

Pull and Replace

My grandfather spent hours working on vehicles. On Saturday mornings and weekday evenings, I'd find him lodged underneath an old Chrysler or bent under the hood of a new Ford. Everyone in town knew him, and if they had a problem with their vehicle, they called Pops. He fixed things. Usually, he fixed things and gave a little unsolicited sage advice along with it. He'd drop a little knowledge nugget in with his repair.

Pops hated foreign cars. He'd work on them, but he'd cuss the whole time. He said they were "cramped, designed for little people with little fingers," and he'd always lament, "You can't rebuild their parts. You have to pull and replace them."

Pops loved old American muscle cars. He'd actually rather rebuild a carburetor than buy a new one. Some parts can be rebuilt; some can't.

I learned Fear couldn't be rebuilt. It was innate and showed up as fear of pain every time. Thus, I stopped working to eliminate the existence of fear, and I began working to replace it when it showed up. With Leon, I feared he'd get bored and abandon me. That fear is still real, but instead of fighting fear, I accept it as a reality and replace it.

Your brokenness kept him around. If you weren't so broken, he wouldn't be interested. You sent off messages that said, "Take me, use me, and I'll keep it crazy!" If you lose the crazy, you'll lose the men. They'll get bored.

When I realize the thought monster runs wildly through my mind, I capture it, and I pull and replace. *Okay, so I'm afraid that if I lose the crazy, I'll lose what makes me special.*

I believe helping people right their wrongs shows them love. Participating in their wrong hurts them. If I continue acting crazy to maintain a harmful relationship, I am not only harming myself, but I am also harming him. Love requires I drop the act. I am happy to lose a relationship that perpetuates harm. I am not alone. I am loved.

In the situation with Leon, I attempted to replace fear with rational love. If I love someone, I cannot participate in their demise, and I must let them go if my relationship hurts them. *And* I am not afraid to be alone because I love them and myself too much.

In this situation, I eventually used my spiritual relationship with God to build me up because I believe He loves me. I confessed what I had done wrong. I made right what I could make right with God and others. Now, I'm telling my story, so others can get right too. I trusted His love more than my fear. Even if I feel abandoned. Simply put, if I replace fear with love, I conquer fear.

Sacrifice

I love memoirs and autobiographies, but a recurring motif gets under my skin. I'll read a memoir, and the author will bemoan her sorrowful, demanding upbringing, and then laud how in later years she became an educated, vibrant contributor to the community and the world at large. Somewhere she'll mention her first marriage, and although she still loves and respects her first husband, the marriage sadly dissipated due to different interests. It all sounds very respectful. Shortly thereafter, a new man rescues her from her woes.

What she doesn't mention is she cheated on her husband with this man; her husband found out, divorced her, and she married husband number two. How do I know? Because she lambasted her parents for twenty chapters but didn't mention her husband's nefarious deeds. Why? He wasn't the one.

Because she can't discretely write, "We grew apart some, so I started screwing this other guy at work, left my husband, and married him." It all falls under the guise of "I respect my ex and that relationship too much to dishonor him because I'm so mature and respectful." Give me a break. You just roasted your parents' life in your book, but you "respect [your] ex too much"? No, you respect yourself. You don't want everyone to know you cheated and your new husband participated in that cheating.

That's one thing I love about certain stories in the Bible. The heroes show their faults. Abraham had a wife and a concubine and married again after his first wife died. He was over a hundred years old! He later kicked his concubine and son out of the house. David had six wives, the first one he locked away in a tower, and later, he killed a man to take his. He also had ten concubines, and his son Absalom slept with all of them. Jephthah sacrificed his daughter. That's right: not himself but his daughter. All the apostles abandoned Jesus, and Jesus' most faithful followers were women. (In those times, it would be embarrassing to admit that the women were more faithful than the men.) Those stories in the Bible show faults. The stories sacrifice the men's reputations for the truth.

I have a sex problem. I used sex for years and years to fill a void it could never fill. I used it to feel loved, excited, accepted; I used it to feed my ego. When I got married, I shriveled sexually. As a result, I connect to illicit love, not explicit love. I can't blame all the men in my past; I have a problem. Although its genesis is rooted in my abuse, I am not exonerated from my behavior. When unworthiness knocks at my door, I must make a decision.

I'll sacrifice. I'll sacrifice my reputation and myself to burn that thought monster up on the altar. When unworthiness comes in the form of Loneliness, I must decide whether to reach out to a blast from the past or to reach out to someone safe. I may confess, "Hey, my thought monster wants to eat me. If they have enough time, I'll be convinced that illicit sex will make me whole again. I don't want to be a slut, so I need some help. Can you talk to me?"

"You've already been a slut."

Ouch. Loneliness tested me to see if I am serious. But I keep going because I need to sacrifice my ego, my need for approval, my unworthiness. Though it seems counterintuitive, describing my weaknesses helps defeat my weaknesses rooted in low self-esteem. But it works as designed. By confessing my weaknesses, I show that my desire to do right exceeds my desire to appear right. In my weakness, I become strong.

Secret Keeper

Invite

Kim and Pam are two friends I met in junior college. They taught me to trust that they could love me without using me, and we could be mutually dependent and mutually independent simultaneously. We could live together, use one another to help each other, and still live our own lives without overstepping boundaries. It was a beautiful mess.

Sometimes we'd throw parties. And we'd invite people over, like one does for parties. We'd also recruit friends to help us decorate, shop, cook, or whatever to prepare for the party. I thought that was crazy. *You don't ask people to help you out with a party you invited them to.* But if you want to party, sometimes you need help. No help. No party.

I learned the same principle held true with the thought monsters. I needed help. I needed an army. An army looked like friends, counselors, authors, speakers, pastors, etc. To divide and conquer, pull and replace, and sacrifice, I invited in other thoughts, perspectives, perceptions, etc. Not to keep me perpetually analyzing and never deciding, but to help me continue being decisive. To choose joy, hope, love, and peace over fear, Doubt, inadequacy, and Loneliness.

Redeem

During the Saturday morning shopping extravaganzas with Momma, we used coupons. For those unfamiliar with physical coupons, they were paper rectangles we redeemed at the store to reduce the price of goods before we used digital coupons. What poor folk called a *turdburg*. Why we called it that, I don't know. Maybe because we thought we were robbing the crap out of the store. Anyway, for the coupon to work, we had to redeem it—give it to the store.

In very much the same way, thought monsters need to be redeemed with an action. At times, I can't drive out a thought with a thought, pull a thought and replace it, or burn the thought up on the altar. Thinking is not enough. Acting makes the change.

When the fear monster attacks, telling me I won't have enough, I might give away more. Doubt whispers, "You've done too many bad things, and nobody will listen to you," so I speak and write more. Perfectionism reminds me I've stolen, so I pay back more than I've taken. Loneliness settles in and keeps me isolated. I get out. I help someone who is lonelier than I am. In doing so, I redeem the thought.

From my past, from what I've done, I realize this isn't always true. I am selfish and I don't combat the thought monsters . . . well, every time. But when I do, I've found that when nothing else works, I must do something. Not from guilt. Not from shame. But from a true desire to defeat the monsters.

Isn't that the point of writing this memoir anyway? I want to discover if digging through my past brings resolve and healing to my present and future. And I want to share. I invite you in. Here's my weight: I've had a lot of bad things done to me, and I've equally done a lot of bad things. Can I get better? Can we get better together? And if everyone turns on us, isn't it an opportunity to grow stronger?

Break Dance

Don't worry. Break's over. Now we can dance. No more tough questions. We'll return to my story and see if I return to me.

Secret Keeper

Analyze

After reading this chapter, I feel

Shree Walker

More Noise

"Sometimes, I feel discriminated against, but it does not make me angry. It merely astonishes me. How can any deny themselves the pleasure of my company? It's beyond me."
—Zora Neale Hurston

I have some more noise to make. I wonder if the little girl inside will ever heal, or if she'll continue making the same mistakes over and over and over. This chapter could be a mistake. When will I ever learn to leave well enough alone?

When I completed the chapter titled "Nobody," I believed I'd finished lamenting my career course in my first school district. I was wrong. I ended the chapter by writing, "Maybe I should make some more noise." Upon further investigation, I discovered I need to make some more noise. For me, and maybe for you. Because we didn't go through all that hell to be mediocre.

Straight Outta Compton

I'm not supposed to be here. There are 3.13 miles between Compton, California, and Watts, California. As I said, I'm from Watts. We make movies about "Straight Outta Compton," we sing songs about being from South Central, and we hear stories about the riots in Watts. I lived there. I remember the riots. I remember walking to school. I shouldn't be here.

Over 70 percent of Americans reside close to the city where they grew up. I'm right back home. I never should have made it out and back. Not being Black. Not knowing poverty. Not after the abuse. Not as a woman. Not being me.

I made a big mistake. A big common mistake. A mistake we're taught to make. I got out, but behaved like I was still in. "Just get your foot in the door, and you can work your way up from there." Right. What if "getting my foot in the door" meant settling for being treated like an undereducated, impoverished, Black female? That's the exact position I put myself in when I joined the public school system.

As I wrote, I joined public education as a substitute, then transitioned into a teacher's position (on a probationary certificate). I did not have my license, so I received a lower compensation than a certified teacher—although I did the same job. After my various promotions, I transferred to the district office. I made a mistake taking that promotion. I should have made more noise.

Equal Pay for Equal Work

I sat in his office waiting, words dancing on the tip of my tongue and decisions whirling in my mind. *What should I do? This isn't what he promised. I didn't work that hard to turn back now.*

"Shree, you will be a specialist over 504 and residential treatment facilities."

"Jim, I got promoted to a coordinator's position. What's the problem? Why am I now a specialist?"

"It's against the policy. See, Rosy is a coordinator, and she'll need to train you, and you will report to her. A coordinator can't report to a coordinator; it's against the policy."

At this time, my youth and inexperience hindered me from saying, "Well, change the dumb policy," so I said, "What will my pay scale be?"

"On par with a specialist."

"So less than what you promised."

"Yes, we can't pay a specialist what we pay a coordinator."

Mistake number one: listening and accepting sheep's wool as the truth. As a result, I got paid less when I got hired. I got paid less when I got promoted. A pattern emerged. They could have promoted Rosy. They could have told me up front I'd be a specialist. They could have changed the policy. They could have had me directly report to someone else and just had Rosy train me. They could have . . . I accepted the position with no more questions asked. I took less. I wasn't supposed to be there anyway.

Rosy the Ripper

I love that old advertisement of Rosy the Riveter from the World War II era. She strikes me as an industrious woman, at one with her strength, willing to lend her resolve and beauty to protect her family, her neighborhood, her nation. She's an inspiration.

I hate the story of Jack the Ripper. He lives in a legend of a single man who committed serial murders in London in the late 1800s. Nobody knows if the murders were linked to a common murderer or if the women murdered were part of a broader hatred of "working" women at the time. Nobody knows if Jack existed or if he was a pseudonym for several men who murdered several prostitutes. Nobody knows why the Ripper ripped so violently and why he hated women so. Maybe Jack was really Jill, and she hated the women her man ran to, so she punished them. Nobody knows.

Rosy and Jack exist as foil characters in the blooms of modern history, but they coexist as one, unique, divided personality I met whom I'll call Rosy the Ripper.

Rosy worked as a coordinator over students with 504 needs and primarily focused on student health. Her desk looked like a train wreck got hit by a cyclone, and neither won. Stacks of manilla folders reached the ceiling and dangled precipitously. More stacks lined the legs of the desk. More lined the walls. Rosy kept records, and the records kept Rosy, and everything kept everything from falling into the paper maelstrom.

She met me with a firm, cold handshake and instantly gave unsolicited advice. "Ms. Walker. Follow my lead. And whatever you do, keep your desk clean." I looked at hers. *Sigh.* She coordinated 504 and I *specialized* in 504—meaning I learned to coordinate 504 trainings and issues while following her lead. And she led.

During the first two weeks in the department, I read and read and read. And I cried, and cried, and cried. *What the hell have I done? I don't know what I'm doing here. And where are the students? This isn't education!* I observed Rosy's mannerisms and became convinced I didn't want to be anything like her, so I tried to make my own way. I had no clue where I was going.

"Shree, get in here."

"Coming."

"You see this email? To whom is this email addressed? What message are you communicating? What legal language are you using to support your decision?"

"The email is to Principal Andrews—"

"Then why isn't his name used in the greeting?"

"I addressed him later in the email, and I—"

"What message are you communicating?"

"I am trying to—"

"Don't *try!* Communicate the message. What do you want them to do?"

"I want them to schedule a meeting with the parent so we can investigate the child's needs to determine what accommodations need to be made instead of just taking the parent's request at face value."

"Then write that verbatim. Don't tiptoe around the issue. They need to know what you want. Now what's the law?"

"No qualified individual with a disability by reason of her disability shall be excluded from the participation in, be denied the benefits of, or be subjected to discrimination under any program or activity receiving federal financial assistance."

"And where should you use that in the email?"

"In the section where I indicate we need to determine if the student is qualified by—"

"Exactly, so quit pussyfooting your emails and lay down the law, literally."

Rosy attended about three or four 504 meetings a year. She focused primarily on student health and keeping me in line. Although Rosy ripped me and my emails to shreds, she taught me that condescending and difficult people make me better. And she made me better. I learned two more things from Rosy: don't let the job consume you, and, in some ways, I wanted to be like her.

Rosy worked late. She worked until nine o'clock some evenings. She worked from home. She worked weekends. She worked herself right into an injury, and she had to leave. She'd been denied her requests so many times that she solved the issue by doing more work. Strong. Beautiful. Determined. Disenfranchised. Rosy later returned, but she left me stronger, wiser, quicker, and with the full responsibility for three departments: 504, residential treatment facilities, and student incident reporting.

Layer the Cake

When I assumed full responsibility for 504, I also got sacked with a report for the Office of Civil Rights. *No big deal. I'm an overachiever. I'll get it done. How bad can it be? I'm not supposed to be here anyway.* Rosy sat cozy on her mandatory sabbatical while I headed up to 504 and gathered the information for this report.

I went to see Betty in HR. "Hey, Betty, how do I get the information for the number of Title IX incidents we had last year?"

"What?"

"The total Title IX incidents."

"Oh. You got sacked with that?"

"What?"

"The Office of Civil Rights report?"

"Yeah."

"The state's been calling about that for weeks."

"And?"

"And they asked me to do it, and I told them, 'No way.'"

"So how do I get the information for Title IX?"

"Use this database, but it's not all collected here. You'll have to call each school separately, speak to the principals."

"All 186."

"All 186."

I called and I hustled. I also hustled over to see Paul in safety and security. "Hey, Paul. How do I know how many bullying incidents and allegations we had last year?"

"Hell if I know."

"Paul?"

"Your department fills out the accident and incident report."

"Yeah, that's for *accidents*. Not for bullying."

"Oh, I slipped and made fun of his mom. Oops! I poked him in the eye! They're all accidents."

"Paul, help me out. I have this report to fill out and—"

Laughter.

"They sacked you with that report, eh? I told 'em to 'get bent' when they asked me."

"I'm sure."

"Call the schools and talk to the lead security office at each campus. He'll get you the information."

"He? At all 186? How many Title IX allegations do you have, Paul?"

"What?"

"Nothing. Have a nice day."

Going to see people seemed like a waste of time, and the 504 burdens needed to be solved too, so I decided to take a shortcut and send an email over to finance.

"Hey, guys, how do I discover what percentage of funds are allocated by demographic?"

Crickets.

"Dear esteemed finance colleagues, due to federal law, I must record and report the district-wide expenditures per demographic, including race, nationality, gender, 504, IEP, and economically disadvantaged status. Please indicate what metric I should use to apprehend this data."

"Hi, Ms. Walker. Sorry you got sacked with that report. We don't have a system that measures that data. You'll have to call all the schools and compile the data yourself."

All 186 schools. When I completed and submitted the twenty-page report, the directors seemed impressed. Apparently, nobody had submitted a completed report, at least not in three years. I'd built the bottom layer of the cake.

Layer 2

I was still a specialist, and 504 looked like a bear. Our documentation lay succinctly at Rosy's desk. Too bad Rosy wasn't there! I advocated for an electronic system. I built all the old data into new electronic forms. I created the trainings for the coordinators at the various schools and the counselors and teachers. I worked to make the trainings mandatory. I facilitated the trainings and had people begging for more. We got the electronic system and drilled into the process of assigning 504 accommodations and meeting the legal requirements—while serving the needs of the students. It took two years.

Icing

I got promoted to a coordinator's position! I also had an administrative assistant assigned to the department. We'd gotten 504 running smoothly, and now we needed to tackle the residential treatment facilities.

Layer 3

The 504 population grew so large that we eventually split it into a north and south region and assigned two coordinators who reported to me. The increase in ADD, ADHD, OCD, and ODD in recent years warranted serious investigation. We built an electronic training system that housed lessons, requirements, and certifications. But while I built that system, and before the two coordinators were added, I worked on the residential treatment fiasco.

When I say *fiasco*, I mean no system existed whatsoever! Whom to pay, when to pay, how to pay? All that had to be answered. Coding the kids in treatment facilities? That fell on Shree. Coding attendance? Shree. Creating a system that tracked the students into and out of RTFs? Shree. Figuring out how to file *thousands* of forms and enter them into an electronic system? Shree. Paying the over two hundred past-due invoices from 2011 when it was 2013, researching the information behind each invoice, creating relationships with those nonplussed clients while training the entire district on the process for residential treatment facilities . . .

Icing

Eventually, I got promoted to supervisor, and we expanded by adding the two additional 504 coordinators whom I mentioned.

Layer 4

"Hello, everyone! Welcome to the student incident and accident report training. I'm Dr. Shree Walker, and I'll be your guide. Today, we'll follow the slogan, "When in doubt, fill it out."

"Uh, Dr. Walker? What about that situation where the kids played in the window over at Oblivious Elementary, and one chopped off his finger? I mean, that happened in like two seconds."

"That's an extreme case. In that situation, we would definitely fill it out."

"What about a kid in my class who sat too far back in his chair? I told him a thousand times to stop, and then he flipped his chair and busted his head."

"Sing it out. When in doubt, fill it out."

"What if a kid falls on the playground?"

"When in doubt . . ."

"What if I jump out my window?"

"Have a student fill it out!"

"Dr. Walker, who's responsible for processing all these forms, contacting the parents, and working with the hospitals, doctors, police, and fire departments?"

"You're looking at her."

"For all 186?"

"All 186."

Icing

I got promoted to director!

Shree Walker

Layer 5

Kids get shoved into foster care for hundreds of terrible reasons. Foster care literally saves lives, but tragic incidents create the need for foster care. For a more exhaustive explanation of the foster care system and my interaction with it in the public school system, please read *Educate Me*. For the purpose of this memoir, I'll keep layering the cake.

Imagine a spiderweb tenuously strung from a doorpost to a light fixture. Myriad strings attach back and forth between the two extremes, and the spider's travel paths are nearly innumerable. So are the eventualities of the foster care system both tenuous and innumerable.

Students land in foster care because their parents died, their sibling died, their parent abandoned them, their parent emancipated them, their foster parents kicked them out, their sibling kicked them out, their grandma died, their aunt or uncle disappeared, etc. One child, two children, three children, four children, sibling sets, cousins, stepsiblings, half-siblings, just found out you're really not my sibling, all the eventualities and scenarios one can imagine occur.

My department accepted the responsibility for foster care. Again, we had to document, train, create an electronic system—cause Lord knows we did everything on paper until I created a system—learn the law; train people on the law; meet with counselors, student services, principals, students, parents, and the juvenile court, office of the court, the department of children's services; create new forms; create FAQs; house sensitive information; attend countless meetings; . . . butter bread, make toast, milk the cow. *Moo*.

Icing

I advocated for and received a raise for the two coordinators who worked with me and the administrative assistant who worked for me. The coordinators received a $20,000 annual raise, while the administrative assistant received a $15,000 raise.

Secret Keeper

Layer 6

"Man, I'll fuck you up! I don't care who you think you is!"
"J.P. Calm down, man. No reason to get violent."
"Man, that bitch stole my shoes. I told you he was—"
"How do you know he stole your shoes?"
"You seen any other yellow Jordans 'round here?"
"How'd you get those in here anyway?"
"Man, I got my resources."
"Look. You calm down and talk to Dr. Walker here about your school, and I'll go see what's up with Case. I'll see if he stole your shoes."
"Man, I don't give a damn about school—"
"Watch your language. You're in the presence of a lady."
"Yeah. Where? All I see's this crusty-ass bitch."
"Mr. Rodriguez. I'm fine. I'll handle J.P. You go handle your business."

That was my welcome to juvenile detention centers (JDC). I experienced many more like it, and many civil yet heart-wrenching ones too. Students moved in and out of JDC like sandpaper. Often, they stayed for ten days and transferred. Sometimes three days, sometimes a year. If the department of children's services ran out of beds, students wound up in JDC. No joke. Even if they didn't do anything wrong. They dressed like, walked like, and behaved like a suspected juvenile criminal. They went to "juvey." Treated like convicts for being a foster child, no wonder they wound up . . . *Tick. Tick. Tick.*

Like at the prior departments, my team had to create, train, modify, systematize, interview . . . I woke up. District handed us all the troubled departments because we handled the trouble. The juvenile detention centers became my baby. I poured myself into the process for the most neglected children, but I also heard the alarm bell ringing. *I don't belong here. Not anymore.* Then the lady who headed the homebound department departed.

Icing

We kept our jobs.

Shree Walker

Layer Seven

Homebound services represent students chronically absent from school due to an illness, syndrome, or disease. Simply put, these students get homeschooled by the district. They stay at home and receive public education. For most homebound students, these services represent a touch of humanity in a tragic world. Some suffer from cancer, and their doctors and teacher represent the only connection they have with the outside world. Others manipulate the system.

We built processes, contacted doctors, talked to the nurse supervisors ... for all 186 schools.

The Icing on the Cake

I love icing. Buttercream's my favorite.

One night, I heard the latch on my backdoor shift. The door opened. I heard footsteps scuttle on the apartment floor. I grabbed the closest thing I could find, a wine bottle. The sound stopped. I stopped. My heart stopped. I peered around the corner, about to make a rush for it, when I spotted myself spooning icing straight from the container to my mouth. One night. Maybe a hundred times.

I need to talk about the icing on the cake. One layer of icing cost me more than I wanted to pay. When I got promoted to the director's position, someone shoved the icing spatula between my shoulder blades. "*Et tu, Brute?*"

A year prior, during our end-of-year presentations, with the lights turned low and summer hopes high, my supervisor clicked to the next slide. My picture and heritage profile with the district splashed the screen, and underneath the subtitle read, "Meet the new director of special populations!"

Applause radiated against the ceiling, and the congratulations deafened me momentarily. I beamed and played it cool, but I'd just checked off another box on my Die Empty list. The week prior, during our year-end barbecue, my supervisor had made the same announcement, although less formally, and without our comprehensive interoffice budget review.

My colleagues congratulated me warmly, one by one, as we left the room that Friday. Two public announcements, two rounds of applause, too much hope.

The following Wednesday, Frank, my supervisor, called me into his office. We discussed the changes in the budget, my new title, salary, and reporting structure. During lunch, I drove to Target and picked up some new patio furniture as a new director. When I returned, he demoted me to supervisor.

"What the hell, Frank? What do you mean I'm not going to be a director?"

"Your obligations and duties are not representative of those of a director."

"No, no, no, no, no. I worked with your number two. I submitted the proposal. You approved it. You announced it at the barbecue last Friday. You pushed it forward. Now you want to tell me that 'my duties are not representative of those of a director?' I've been doing a director's job for the past two years."

"I'm sorry, Shree. There's nothing I can do."

"Who said?"

"HR."

"What's HR got to do with it? They said we submit the proposal, and then we create the position. They just approve."

"Upon further review, they decided the details of the job—"

"You and I both know that's a lie! What are you going to do about it? That's bull. I know that's bull!"

"There's nothing I can do."

"So you can get a raise for my teammates, for my admin assistant, but you can't do this?"

"My hands are tied."

"It's in the budget. We made the announcement."

"My hands are tied."

"This is some bull . . ."

"My hands are tied."

Shree Walker

A Rose for Me?

In William Faulkner's short story "A Rose for Emily," the main character, Emily, befriends a man named Homer Barron. The townsfolk believe they are lovers but are perplexed because Homer "liked men."[3] But the couple courted on Sunday evenings and took long buggy rides together. Some nights, Homer snuck into Ms. Emily's home.

When people found Homer's dead body thirty years later, Emily had been sleeping with it the whole time! And she'd poisoned him with arsenic. I wonder if she baked it into a cake for him, maybe a seven-layer cake.

A year after being publicly humiliated by the demotion-promotion, I scoured emails at my desk. The decision didn't sit right with me. The explanation confused me. I *felt* like someone had poisoned my cake. Then I found it.

"Frank, remember last year when you said your hands were tied for the promotion?"

"Yeah. That was awful. One of the worst days of my professional career. To offer a promotion and then take it back the same day. That's terrible."

"I know. You know what's worse?"

"What?"

"I found the email from HR. It said, 'The decision is yours.'"

"Oh, I'm sure you misunderstood. Send me that email."

"Sent."

But Frank made the decision instead. He decided that keeping the extra funds in the budget outranked me, so he told HR, "I'll just embarrass the hell out of her publicly, stab her in the back, and then blame you. Sound good?" They agreed. He humiliated me and kept it going for a year. His hands weren't tied because he busied them stabbing me in the back or baking me a fake celebration cake! Needless to say, I got promoted. Not because of his ruse but because of my work.

Frank loved adding the layers, but he hated spreading the icing. When the icing ran thin, rather than buying more, they bought arsenic instead.

---

[3] William Faulkner and M. Thomas Inge, "A Rose for Emily" (Columbus: Ohio, Merrill, 1970),

But unlike Emily, who fed it to Homer, they fed *me* to the rat. Smiling all the while.

I Don't Belong Here

I made a mistake. I thought, *I don't belong here*, and allowed my gratitude to spoil into a grotesque misunderstanding of boundaries. Boundaries keep the wolves out and the sheep in. And the shepherd controls the gate. I'd transformed from a sheep to a shepherd, but I still behaved like a sheep. I'd become indentured to the idea that I didn't belong. But I did belong. Not because of me, but because of the work. The work spoke for itself.

And that's the real reason I left. The ignorance, the sleights, the excuses, and the bureaucracy all played a part, but in the end, I left because I made a mistake. I esteemed myself too lowly and didn't realize when I outgrew the sheepfold. The time came for this girl to protect some new sheep.

I guess I've made enough noise. For now.

Shree Walker

Evaluate

Before reading this chapter, I thought

After reading this chapter, I now think

Flannel Graph

On lonely nights, shepherds told stories and counted stars. Aspiring to understand the complexities of the universe while grappling with the infirmities inflicted by nature and its raw powers, shepherds rehearsed stories to inspire, to infuriate, to initiate, and to laugh. The laughter allowed them to exhale the breath of life, the joy stored within. Stories kept them sane through the long nights of keeping sheep. The stories protected their minds and spirits while they protected others.

Thinking of sheep and shepherds, I remembered Sunday school. As a child, when we attended church, we marched downstairs to Sunday school first. The teacher huddled us into a story room. Paintings of famous biblical stories and characters lined the walls. She fed us cookies there and, ironically, red Kool-Aid.

On special occasions, she mesmerized us with the flannel graph. Cotton-ball-covered sheep followed terry-cloth-covered shepherds into a pen. Eventually, one sheep escaped, headed for the dastardly cliff. Oh, but a cotton-covered wolf infiltrated the pen, behaving like a sheep but surveying them like a Golden Corral. Swooping in, the shepherd destroyed the wolf and rescued the sheep from becoming lambchops.

I often wondered, *Shouldn't the wolf eat the sheep so they can join the Great Shepherd in heaven?* Short-lived pain traded for eternal glory—the teachers never taught that. Anyway, what a good experience the shepherds had. They watched sheep. They killed wolves. And they were heroes.

I, too, have some stories. A few short stories about some sheep, some wolves, and the search for a shepherd. But figuring out who's who always proved difficult for me.

The Wolf

"That's 'Doctor.' Like I said, you can't dress up Gerald as James and get the same treatment for Gerald as you do James. We must follow the law." I sat back in my chair, satisfied, a little pregnant with pride, but convinced I'd done the right thing. I'd been called into a meeting at one of our charter schools to advise them on how to handle a 504 situation with a disgruntled parent, and so far, they'd been handled.

Assigning 504 accommodations is a tricky business. Since the uptick in impairments such as ADD, ADHD, and the like, more and more parents have suggested accommodations for self-diagnosed children. By *self-diagnosed*, I mean the parents diagnose the children themselves. But that's not the way it works.

For a student to receive a 504 accommodation in the past, a doctor made a diagnosis. Thus, more parents advocated for diagnoses, and more doctors diagnosed patients with more impairments that substantially limit a child's learning. Educators too. If students didn't understand their school assignments, rather than dig in, educators searched for diagnoses. More for less.

That's not true anymore. Now a doctor's diagnosis is requested, not required. A variety of sources can make a 504 determination. It's no longer a diagnosis but a determination based on observable behaviors that may include a diagnosis. More areas of gray. More obscure. More human.

Adding more ingredients to the witch's brew, in our district, we served not only the public schools but also the charter schools—and the charter schools were beasts. One distinguishing factor of a charter school is parent choice. For instance, geography mandates a student's school in the public school system, but parents choose the location in the charter system. And some try choosing everything else.

Mama, a wealthy, forty-something white woman, who stepped out of *Desperate Housewives* in an eye-popping white blouse and too-tight denim jeans and high heels, tapped her French tip nails on the side of her recycle-friendly coffee cup. Guess which coffee company she purchased it from?

Trying to appease Mama, the charter school rushed through the process. She asked for more. The charter school gave more. She asked again and tapped her cup with her trigger finger.

The charter school called me. "Dr. Walker, we don't know how to handle this situation. Mama asks for more and more accommodations—ones that don't even make sense—and she's never satisfied."

A quick side note. In education, we often use titles: Mr., Ms., Mrs., or Dr. We even list our credentials in our email signature. I don't like it, but whatever. In the real world, I don't call every reverend "Reverend" or every master plumber "Master." And neither does the media nor anyone else. I did a television interview once, and they called me "Shree," not "Dr. Shree," because I'm not a medical doctor. What difference does it make? I know I went to school.

At Harvard, where I did a study, nobody called anybody "Doctor." One self-aggrandized student audaciously questioned it: "Why don't we call one another 'Doctor' here? It is Harvard, after all."

"Because everyone in this room is a doctor. It's understood. It is Harvard, after all."

Mama continued tapping. And since Mama wasn't happy, she ain't gonna let nobody be happy. At the onset of the 504 meeting, an imperative we observe is introductions. We introduce ourselves around the room, so each participant keenly understands the nature of each participant's presence. When my turn came, I said, "I'm Shree Walker, the director of 504 and special populations for Metro Nashville Public Schools." The position title was an imperative; the educational one was not. Still tapping.

"Ms. Mama, to assign any additional accommodations—or any for that matter—it's imperative that we collect information to appropriately address the needs of the student. We have sixty days. You filed this request six days ago."

"It's imperative that Gerald receive these accommodations. He needs extra time on tests, all the information read aloud, and his test questions should require no greater than a sixth-grade reading level to comprehend. I know my rights. Don't you agree, Sherry?"

"Ms. Mama—"

"It's missus."

"Mrs. Mama, reducing the reading level is a modification, not an accommodation, and modifications are reserved for students with an IEP, students who have an impairment that hinders their functioning, which then qualifies them for special education services. Gerald does not have that."

"Sherry. I know my son. I know my rights. He needs these accommodations."

"Mrs. Mama, what impairment does Gerald have that warrants these changes?"

"He has ADD."

"That's on James's paperwork. The paperwork indicates—"

"Excuse me, Dr. Walker, may I see that paperwork?"

"Of course, Michael," I said. Michael, the 504 coordinator for that site, missed Mama's sleight of hand.

"Let me continue. The paperwork indicates Gerald suffers from sleep apnea, which may qualify him for extra time on tests, but not for all information to be read aloud or for modified tests or reduced assignments or modified curricula in any of his classes."

"You're from the public schools. Not the charter schools. Why are you here anyway?"

"In our system, the public schools provide support for the charter schools—"

"Gerald's going to have these accommodations. My husband is friends with the president of the school board. I know my rights. What's your position anyway? I don't even know whether to call you miss or missus." But she said it all drawn out, like *missrezzz*!

I said, "Neither. That's 'Doctor.'"

I heard a growl in the distance.

Sheep

"Priscilla missed eighty-seven days during the last school year, recording stints of twenty consecutive days, thirteen consecutive days, nine consecutive days, and a whopping thirty-one consecutive days, and others sprinkled in here and there for good measure. We only have 180 days to work with. Somebody tell me how she was promoted from tenth grade to eleventh grade."

"Dr. Walker, you know that chronic absenteeism majorly disrupts students' education, but we can't control physical maladies."

"I know, Mr. Spurgeon, but we don't have a diagnosis listed. We have a student who is chronically absent and often out-of-state."

"Ms. Walker?"

"Yes."

"Can't we best meet Priscilla's needs by providing homebound services?"

"Where is her home?"

"I don't know, Ms. Walker. But I know she isn't just skipping." She peered at me over the top of her readers, her graying hair pulled back loosely.

"Mrs. Reynolds, I understand, but we have a burden of proof to meet. A burden of proof that indicates Priscilla belongs in our school district. If she runs away, she should be listed as a runaway. Where is Allen anyway?"

"Ms. Walker, Principal Starks had a prior commitment."

"What about Priscilla's parents?"

"They, too, couldn't make it, Ms. Walker."

"We scheduled this meeting without the key stakeholders in the room, without anybody with any authority to do anything about the situation?"

"No, Ms. Walker. We can do what is in the best interest of the child."

"It would be in her best interest to attend school. I suggest we unenroll her, and she needs to reenroll in the school district where she resides. She's missed the first thirty days of school this year, and the records indicate she doesn't live in the state."

"Ms. Walker, that's a little harsh, don't you think?"

"Excuse me," Stephanie, a much younger white girl fresh out of college, slapped her hand on the table. "Mrs. Reynolds, it's Dr. Walker."

Mrs. Reynolds, who looked like Stephanie's grandmother, turned bright red. I tapped Stephanie on the leg, leaned in, and whispered just loud enough to be heard around the room, "She knows, but we just gonna let her be great today anyway." Mrs. Reynolds's face brightened even further, like a cherry bomb about to explode.

We continued the meeting, but I swear I heard a sheep in the distance. A very white, white sheep.

Shepherd

My love languages funnel into one: quality time. In relationships, I want to go deep. All the way to the bone. To the core. I'm searching for a person's soul, not the mirage covering the dressing screen, but the unhusked core beneath. I want to experience and experience fully, with no condemnation. That's where the search for the shepherd arises, from the desire to know and be fully known. To be protected from what harms me, even if I am the culprit. Maybe that's a fantasy or a mirage itself.

I picture Adam and Eve, free and naked in the garden, but that happened *before* they acquired the knowledge of good and evil. Is there a shepherd who can see me for me—all the good and all the evil—and to clothe me and protect me from my own devices?

I don't know. The search continues.

In education, I didn't find any shepherds. I found sheep, wolves, and teachers. Many teachers, administrators, parents, and the like acted like shepherds, but when the rubber met the road, I often found them retreating to protect themselves. That's human nature. Were they not shepherds or just not good shepherds?

I fought the wolves and protected the sheep, but I didn't always get it right. I also followed sheep at times, and I also followed wolves. Did my personal battles that so starkly contrasted with my professional behavior disqualify me from the position of a shepherd? Was I a sheep, a wolf, and a shepherd?

I'm sorry that I didn't find any shepherds. I don't have any stories about them. Oh well, Halloween comes soon. I'll dress up as one.

Secret Keeper

Shepherd Leads, Shepherd Leaves

I love autumn in Nashville. The leaves change colors and fall to the ground, and we rake them in piles like a ritual inaugurating the winter. Before we bag the leaves, I enjoy noticing the contrasting shapes of the colors and hues, forming the artist's expression of change. The bits and pieces of leaves represent the deep-rooted tree that shed them. I haven't found a whole shepherd, but I've found bits and pieces that represent the real thing. I think the bits are the best it gets, and when the season changes, I bag them up and leave them in the past.
  Like I do.

Shree Walker

Create

After reading this chapter, I will restore myself by

Sheep, Wolf, Shepherd: Part 1

"Living your naked truth will always disturb those living well-dressed lies."

—Unknown

He sprinted through the road wearing nothing but plaid-checkered pants and red Converse sneakers, a golden-brown body, shredded from sternum to waistline. His silky, black hair whistled in the wind like a scene from *The Last of the Mohicans*. I'd descended the stairwell from my apartment and drunk in the cool water. He jostled by me, briefly saluting, and bounded up the stairs. *Who was this bad boy with that bad bod?*

His name was Ja. Like Ja Rule, but unlike Ja Rule, he was *never on time*. That's why he sprinted through the road—not on the side or sidewalk, or crosswalk like a normal person—he ran in the middle. That day he ran late. He had a job interview with Sprint and fifteen minutes to make it. He never did.

Not in fifteen minutes, anyways. Late, as usual, he wore the same plaid-checkered pants, with a silk shirt and sneakers, again. This time, Jordans—before they were too vintage. How do I know? I worked at Sprint too. (I wasn't a teacher. Not yet.) I didn't have to look far to find Ja, only on the job.

Shree Walker

Wolf?

Ja looked like a wolverine: hard body, tattoos, scruffy, piercing eyes, sharp jaw, intense. A beautiful Black man, Ja's skin appeared light, but his heart was dark. Edgy. The manager told me he "was scary and enchanting" when she hired him. Like a dream catcher. Wolverines are known to fight to the bitter end and attack any opponent. They don't back down.

Ja never backed down. I know. When I met him, he had a girl named Sharee. Like me, but spelled differently. They fought and fought often, and that relationship tore quickly, but it held together through the tugged arms of his son. Finally, she had to go. It was his son, not hers. He pursued me.

I'd seen what I wanted, but I wasn't itching for a fight, so I stayed away. I'm not afraid of a wolf or wolverine, but I'd seen too much. One too many dogfights for me.

Sheep?

"Ja, when are you going to renew your license? You know you can't stay here forever with a Georgia license."

"I know Sh-ree, but I hate that bureaucratic, governmental spying. They don't need to know all my whereabouts."

"Ja, what's the truth?"

"Okay, I'm afraid of the DMV. I can't deal with all those people asking me all those questions. I always fill out the forms wrong. They treat me like I'm stupid."

"Want some help?"

"No, I'll take care of it."

He never did. Things like that, he never did. He let his license expire; he let his insurance forms lay idly in his apartment. He let his cell phone bills pile up, even though he worked at Sprint.

I loved how he said my name, "*Sh-ree*." Not every time, but most times. He didn't draw it out; he said it with conviction and passion—like he knew what it meant. *Shree* is Hindi; it means "prosperity, radiance, beauty." It seemed like he could find the intrinsic value in me but couldn't muster the self-capital to value and take care of himself.

Ja made music. He recorded music, mixed music, played the drums and piano, and promoted musicians. His apartment ballooned with music from the forties to the present day. CDs and vinyl played, often Eric Roberson and Dwele—the *Hold On* album—continuously. His vitality presented a hard, brutal character dressed in an outlandish fashion that worked only for him. Not trendy, but authentic—he built a wardrobe and look that hybridized fierce with aloof.

He was a sheep. Inside that grown body existed a little boy who pined for love and acceptance.

"Here you go, Sh-ree. I made a card for you."

"For me, you made a card for me?"

"Yeah. For your birthday."

"Let me see it. What is a zebra without stripes? How can one fly a kite without wind? What is a beach without sand? What good is a lesson plan without a teacher? What do you call a class without students? NOTHING! Good morning, Denise! I bet you are wondering why I left this card black and white, huh? Well, to be honest, I didn't have time to do much else, so I let it be what it is. I listed some things that are beautiful enough without all the additions. Simply put, you make life colorful and bright. Sunshine. You are water to roots. Thanks for helping me grow, Queen! Happy birthday, Shree Denise Walker!'"

"Yeah."

"Yeah?"

"Yeah. You know, you should be my wife, my forever bride. Will you marry me?"

"Ja, this is so sweet, but you can't take care of yourself. How are you going to take care of me?"

Shepherd?

He never did. He never did leave me. We listened to music for hours, speaking of our hurts and fears. We played cards and dreamed our dreams. He wanted to build a music studio where he could record musicians and help them climb to the top.

"The system is dumb. All the world's greatest musicians go unnoticed because we don't care about talent or charisma or genius behind the strings and voice. We care about marketing—getting noticed—not what moves a person's soul."

"Why do you say that?"

"Walk around Nashville. Step inside some bar or listen on the street corner, and you'll hear musicians bellowing songs with soul that move you to your core. You'll want to follow them home, worship the ground they touch, but you'll never see them get a record deal."

"Maybe they're not that good. Just that good to you."

"Nah. They don't strive, not for marketing anyway. They strive for their music, to transfer their being into the beats."

"Or they're afraid to be rejected, so they don't pursue what's theirs to take."

"You don't understand. You never will."

Stubborn and persistent, he pursued. He pursued me. Like a shepherd, he tried to protect me.

"Ja, I couldn't keep him off. I've never told anybody this part, but I couldn't keep him off. He pushed me down, broke me down, and held me there. I counted the fish between my waterfall tears. I cried, but nobody heard me. Nobody came to rescue me."

"Shree, I'm so sorry. Your heart wanted out, but your body couldn't follow, so it protected you. I'm so sorry. I'm here for you. I'm here. I'll never leave."

He never did. I bore my soul to that man like no man before, and he guarded my heart and my body. He told me about red cardinals. "When you see a red cardinal, you know that somebody is looking down from above, watching over you."

Goodbye

Ja and I developed a soul tie that transcended time and locale. But eventually, I left. I didn't leave him or Nashville, but I moved into education and out of love with him. We could never be. I needed a shepherd, and he straddled the fence between wolf and sheep. I moved into a relationship with another man and moved out of the apartment complex.

He moved back to Chicago, and we said our goodbyes.

"I will always love you, Ja."

"And when I look to the moon or the sun, I'll see you. I love you, Shree."

We continued to keep in contact over the years. He later spiraled into drugs. He FaceTimed once and showed me his buck fifty, which is 150 stitches. A scar requiring 156 stitches spanned his face. Alive, but barely breathing, he crawled to help and was rushed to the hospital. He called me three months later, and that's when he bore his scar. I'd borne mine to him too.

I have long believed in angels with scars and monsters with friendly faces.

He moved again, to Hawaii, then Kentucky, and back to Chicago. He visited me in Nashville, and I told him about my boyfriend. Ja asked me when he'd get a chance. "Next life, love," I quoted. "Next life."

My mind wouldn't let him go. *I need to call Ja. I need to call Ja.* I sat busily answering emails, but my mind wouldn't leave me alone. *Call Ja. Call him now!* When my loud mind disrupts my silent work, I've learned to listen. I called Ja. Wrong number. Probably cut off from an unpaid bill.

I used Google. I found his son. Arrested. I searched again, searched through my past, digging for something I shouldn't find, until I found Ja's obituary.

Goodbye.

Shepherd

When I lace up my red Converses and tie them tight, I imagine them as emblematic cardinals, walking with me wherever I go. I don't look for the red cardinals; they come with me, reminding me that somebody watches over me from above.

I hear the Good Shepherd has scars too. I've wondered if he'd take his scarred hand and hold mine, and we could walk this out together. Why did he keep his scars? Why not heal them completely? I guess the scars show the work, and the sheep need to see them to believe . . . I guess.

I hope Ja knows. I hope they traded stories and Ja's been shepherded in, guarded from the wolves. We'll keep fighting down here and leave it to the Shepherd to know the difference.

Shree Walker

Apply

Because of my experience reading this chapter, now I will

Sheep, Wolf, Shepherd: Part 2

"We didn't know how to love each other through our own brokenness."
—Shree Walker

His hand caressed my shoulder. I flinched under the weight of its light touch. I held my breath. *Here it comes. Oh no! Here it comes.* I raced to the bathroom, locked the door, and fell to my knees. With the towel, I covered my screams, suffocating. I rocked back and forth as the tears rolled to the floor, and my mind replayed every touch.

"He used me. He used me. He used me. He used my body as his playground and my heart as his clean-up cloth!" I jumped at the knock at the door.

"Shree?"

"Yeah, David. I'm sorry. I'm so sorry."

"Who are you talking to in there?"

"Myself. David, I'm sorry. I started thinking about it again."

"Okay, I'm here. I'll be ready when you come out."

I held the towel more tightly. "God, what is wrong with me? Why can't I make love to my husband? Why do I do this?" When I came out of the bathroom hours later, David slept soundly beneath the covers.

"David, you asleep?"

"No, Re. I'm up."

"I'm sorry."

"What's going on?"

"I can't get still. When you touched me, it took me back."
"It's okay. Let's get some sleep. I love you."
"Okay. I love you too."

Withdrawn

He rubbed his hand on my face, down my neck, toward my breasts. I closed my eyes. My mind wandered. *Where am I? Am I here?* I opened my eyes. David. I leaned in, hugged him, and he continued. He unbuttoned my shirt. Eyes closed. *Where am I?*

I backed away and readjusted. It started. *Do I keep my eyes open, or do I close them? Leon? Brian? No Name? No. No. No! No more lists.*

"Shree, what's wrong? Where'd you go?"

I sat up straight, pressed my back against the headboard. He searched my eyes, but the blankness inside me stared back.

"Shree?"

I curled up in a ball, pulling my knees to my chest, and lay on my side. "No, David. Not tonight. Please don't touch me. I can't. I'm so sorry."

"It's okay. Let's get some sleep. I love you."

"I love you too."

I cried myself to sleep.

Sex Is Emotional

"No, David. Not tonight."

"What's wrong?"

"When you touch me, when we make love, I feel inadequate. This feeling comes over me. I don't know. It owns me. I told you that I learned to disassociate. Now I can't reconnect with my own body. I feel like I'm not good enough."

"But I'm telling you that you're good enough."

"It doesn't work that way. I feel inadequate. Nothing you say changes my mind."

"We never had this problem when we were dating. You were all about it then."

"But we were dating."

"What's that got to do with it?"

"I don't know. I don't know. I don't know. How can I explain how I feel? I felt sexy, like a performance. Now I feel like a child. I don't know my own body."

"Shree. It's just sex. We've done it hundreds of times."

"I know. My heart's in it. I swear. But this feeling comes over me, and I can't get my body to move with me. David, the body keeps the score."

"At least someone gets to."

"What'd you say?"

"Nothing. It's okay. I'm here. I'll hold you. I'm here."

"Thank you. I love you."

"I love you too."

PTSD

The semi's tire blows, the amputee swerves his car to the side of the road, slams the brakes, hits the floor, and yells, "Down, down, stay down." He's alone in his car with his sweat and his nightmares. The enemy crawls through his mind, coming for him, seeking his life. His internal warrior asks, "Do I stay down? Do I escape? Put it in gear. Let's go!"

He thrusts himself back in the driver's seat, tugs his good leg over the shifter, and presses the brake pedal. The rearview mirror shows another eighteen-wheeler bearing down on him. Before his mind connects to his body, he slams the vehicle in gear and presses the accelerator to the floor. Too late.

David climbed on top of me. I leaned up, yielding myself to him. He pressed his lips on my neck. The bomb exploded. I pulled back. "Get off me! Get off me! Get off me!'"

"Shree, what the hell?"

"David?"

"I'm here. I'm here."

"David. I'm sorry. I'm so sorry."

"I'm here."

"David, I think I have PTSD."

"What?"

"I'm like the wounded veteran. When you touch me, I'm back in Iraq or Beirut, crawling through the dirt."

"What the hell are you talking about?"

"I think I have PTSD."

"I thought you said you could disassociate. Do that now. Disassociate."

"I can't control it."

"Control it for me. C'mon. Do you need me to pretend to be a police officer or a cowboy? What do I need to do to get my wife back?"

"I need you to listen to me. To hurt with me, to feel for me."

"Who hurts with me?"

"David, I hurt with you."

"Seems like you hurt with yourself."

"David!"

"I mean it. All this 'protect me, protect me' garbage, yet I'm here for you every day. Every night I come home, and you're happy until we go to bed. Hell, now you are mad or sad or something when you hit the door. You say, 'It's not you, it's me,' but what about me? Do I just let you kick me off?"

"I don't know. I don't know, David. I don't—"

"Know. I know."

"Well, what do you want to do?"

"Have sex."

"David."

"Let's get some sleep. I love you."

"I can't sleep now."

"Okay. I'll get some sleep. I love you."

Running Through My Mind

I'm going to do it this time. I'm going to stay present. I got this. When is that report due? How many people do we need to invite next week? Where's David's son? Stop it. Shree, pay attention. Remain present. Make love to your husband. Maybe if I play a movie in my mind. He's married. He's got kids. He's left her. He chose me. He chose me for tonight. I'm engaged. I'm engaging. I'm fading. What the hell? What the hell is wrong with me? God, why can't I be intimate with my husband? But . . . I can. I've done this before. I'll be Frank. Why am I thinking about Frank? I don't like Frank. He lied to me. He lied. He lied . . .

"Shree!"

"Huh?"

"Look at me."

His expression said it all. "Where are you? Where did you go? You don't love me. What's wrong with you?"

Good question. What's wrong with me?

Abused Abuser

They say the abused often becomes the abuser. Had I become my husband's abuser, enticing him into prison, shackling him with the ball and chain, and stepping behind the wall to watch him writhe? He was right. We had no problem with intimacy when we dated.

I've had a lot of sex. I've had a lot of sex with a lot of men, so this mutiny in my body took its repressed anger out on its victim. In this situation, the victim was David. The abused now abused and punished David at night for a lifetime of wrongs I had experienced. *Welcome to my prison. Here, I give you all you want until I lock the cell, then I'll torture you. To death.* I've had a lot of sex.

Was I the monster in the room? The one with the pretty face. Unless . . . *it was Mr. Pain!* The fear monster struck again, holding us hostage in his fell clutch. I had to let David go. I was killing him. Well, Mr. Pain was killing us.

I was finally safe and now I couldn't be safe.

Fear

"Describe the fear to me."

"I'm afraid there is something else going on, that she's not telling me the truth. Like, she's got another man, and she's spending all her energy entertaining him, so when she comes home, she's spent. She's got nothing left for me. I don't believe her."

"Good, David, you told me about the fear, but you didn't describe the fear. Let's try with Shree."

We went to counseling. *Famous last words.* Everybody says that, but how many people actually do the work the counselor ascribes? I'd venture to say way less than 10 percent. David and I tried to work though the issues, but we couldn't manage.

"Shree, describe the fear."

"I can't connect. I don't have a fantasy running in my mind, so I feel inadequate, unable to connect with David through my body. I just want to be held, eat ice cream together, play cards together, things like that. You know, quality time. I want to connect with my husband, but I can't. Not physically, not now."

"You told me about the fear, but you didn't describe it. Are you afraid he'll leave you? Are you afraid you're not enough? Too much? Describe what it feels like."

"I'm in a whirlpool, sinking down, down, down. I reach for help, but I can't grab anything. My hands keep slipping. I'm drowning. The waves crash on me. I hold my breath. I pop up for air, and a wave crashes. Water on my lungs. Can't breathe. Can't get out. Can't get my mind and body to do what I want them to do, so I kick and flail like a child throwing a tantrum, and that pulls me under. I'm mad. I'm scared. I want to tear myself apart. I want to give up and just go under, but my body won't let me do that either. It wants to fight, and I just want to be at peace. And then I'm floating on the water calmly, but I can't find David."

"It's actually quite common."

"What is?"

"Disassociation during sexual intimacy. Shree, your case is extreme because of your trauma, but the racing thoughts and feelings of being disconnected are common."

"In women," David commented.

"In everybody. Men and women both struggle with sexual intimacy. Especially if they have been promiscuous or abused, but even if they've only had one partner. Some of it is personality; if the person exhibits anxiety and worry, then they're more likely to allow their mind to wander. Some men wander off to what they call their 'highlight reel.' Some women make their grocery list. It's common, and it's seasonal."

Secret Keeper

"What do you mean by seasonal?"

"Shree, a person can have a partner for fifty, sixty, even seventy years. Do you believe that the sex is great the entire time? What if a spouse loses his job, or they have a fourth child, or any number of issues arise? Sexual intimacy connects to peace."

"What about before we were married?"

"Were you intimate?"

"Yes, sexually."

"Did you trust each other with yourselves more than your body?"

"Kinda. I'm not sure anymore."

"You need to heal and be patient. It's a process, but I promise: it's seasonal.

Little Girl Within

I couldn't wait to start. I bought the workbook *Healing the Wounded Heart* by Dan Allender and dove right in. I took weekend trips to a local hotel to sit with myself, and to invite the little girl within to participate in the healing with me. David would visit me, and we would go on a date, eat some ice cream, talk, and grow together.

We made appointments with the counselor, did some work, and worked together to grow back into love. But the little girl within came out when we tried to be intimate. She said, "Hey! It's me. You forgot about me! I am not comfortable with this. Don't touch me!"

I asked David to wait for me, and he did. He struggled through the late nights, prayed with me, protected me, loved me—but for how long, David? How long? The little girl whispered, "He won't stay. They never do."

"David, it's like arrested development. I stopped growing. The little girl stopped growing, and I'm handcuffed to my past."

"I understand," he said. "I'll wait for you."

Wolf, Sheep, Shepherd

In human history, no shepherd outranks David in bravery, courage, or fame. Known for slaying lions, giants, and bears, he stands alone, atop the heap of sheep protectors. Famed for his aim with stones, David slung himself from shepherd to warrior, to fugitive, to king. Meanwhile, he practiced polygamy, adultery, murder, and returned to fugitive status. Apparently, his heart mattered, and in his heart, he was both bold and contrite.

My David was too. While dealing with my storm of anticlimactic behavior after we married, he held me both tightly and loosely. Tightly enough to keep me close, and loosely enough to allow me to breathe. Until I needed more. Then he cracked.

David and I both needed to heal. We both had a past that haunted us, albeit differently, and we connected through our own brokenness. And our own brokenness tore us apart.

Shepherds slay wolves to protect sheep. Then they harvest wool and eat sheep. For all their protection and self-sacrifice, shepherds, too, guard their self-interests. They lay down their lives for their sheep, but the sheep lay down their lives for their shepherds. A mutual contingency exists. And I can't tell which is which. I don't know if I was the sheep, the shepherd, or the wolf. David doesn't know, either. We played our parts: we laid down our lives, and we found someone worth protecting together.

We had no children. I had mine at school; he had his from a previous marriage, but we had none together. We saw the writing on the wall, the writing pointing us in one mutual direction. Papa-Dad.

Secret Keeper

Understand

My experience reading this chapter was

Shree Walker

Failure

Feeling loved and feeling sad, I love you Papa-Dad. David's mother had died several years earlier. A beautiful woman, she called me Kelly, and I called her my archangel because of the inverted arch that beamed from her face every time I saw her. David's father, Papa-Dad, lived alone after his wife passed. Growing old, he needed more help, and who better to help him than two shepherds who couldn't tend their own sheep?

I loved Papa-Dad. A kind and generous man, he always had time for me. We moved in with him, so we could help him after his wife died.

"How's my Shree doing today?"

"Good, Papa-Dad! How are you?"

"I'm good. Lonely here when you're gone, but good. Those boys at school giving you any trouble?"

"Papa-Dad, now you know I don't work with the students all day long anymore. I'm cramped in an office, dealing with politics."

"How's the swamp?"

"Full. And sticky."

"Good. I made spaghetti tonight with Papa-Dad's famous meatballs."

"Let me guess. Pork ribs."

"You got it. Why eat meatballs when you can have ribs?"

"I don't know. I guess that's what the Italians liked."
"Good thing I ain't Italian!"
"Or liked."
"You know, from the day I met you, you've been all right by me."
"Cause I brought you candy and peanuts!"
"Cause you're you. I don't ever have to worry about you because I know I'm getting the real you."
"I don't know, Papa-Dad. Sometimes . . ."
He gave me a look that said, *Whatever I say is final on the matter, and you don't have to accept it, but you can't change my mind.*
"I know what I see."

Feeling Loved, Feeling Sad

Living with Papa-Dad made me both happy and sad. I experienced more contentment, safety, and love in that house than at any time I can remember. He treated me like his daughter, and I ate it up. Even watching the news with him was an event!

But my life proved that rainbows don't last forever. Weird how the sunshine brings out the rainbow after the rain. I'd go to work, crush it, and come home feeling sad. Depression ransacked me like an open-door 7-Eleven. I pumped the good things in, and it pilfered them right back out through the back door.

David and I quit attempting to be intimate. Then he quit altogether. He didn't give up on me, but he stopped pursuing me. Dates stopped. Dating stopped. Late-night conversations about hopes and dreams stopped. Crying continued. Brick walls continued. Depression continued. And something new started: detachment. David and I detached.

I went to work; he went to work. I came home; he came home. We met with Papa-Dad, but we didn't meet with each other. Our conversations consisted of talking about our problems or not talking at all. I decided to crush it.

Shree Walker

Crushing It

All the while, I crushed it at work. I avoided the pull to slip into a humdrum, thinking about a job I could do in my sleep. I pushed for clarity and finality in the process for the juvenile detention centers. I scored the raises for my department. I left it all on the table. But for all the grit and grind I produced at work, for all the conflicts I resolved, I couldn't resolve the one within me. So I departed.

Separated

My work life and personal life came to a crossroads that didn't represent the other. I felt divided, like a dichotomy of put-together and falling apart. I loved David, and I loved Papa-Dad, but I had to go.

I leased my own apartment. When I stepped out, I achieved some clarity. A mutiny existed in my body; I knew that. I tried to release the protective armor, but it was stitched to my skin.

David loved me, but he didn't want to do the work. Loving a person who's been abused takes incredible patience, and he didn't have it any longer. The more love I received, the more depressed I became. He didn't understand. Couldn't understand. Didn't want to deal with his own brokenness to see why he couldn't turn toward me in my deepest pain. Why he pulled away? I felt depressed when I received love because I wasn't searching for it anymore. And the search made it special. The search made me special. And that's all I ever wanted to be.

In relationships, our struggles often unearth the struggles of our partners. I offered this sacred ground, the broken core of me, but he feared it. I turned inward. *Am I too much? Am I asking too much? Am I not enough? Am I not enough to meet his needs?*

I wanted to date David.

"Pick me up from my apartment at 7:30."

"Shree, this is stupid. I'm your husband, and I have to set an appointment to see you? I can't just kiss you? I have to wine and dine you just to be with you? This is foolish."

"It's better than yelling, fighting, and cheating."

"It's childish."

"What do you mean?"

"Kids date. We don't date to get married to date again. We date to get married to be married. To show our love for each other and to be there for each other—through thick and thin."

"You can show your love to me by dating me."

"And you can show your love to me by sleeping with me. But you can't. Right? Isn't that what you said? 'David, I can't, not tonight, I can't.' How is it I say, 'I can't date you,' and that's not good enough, but you say, 'I can't screw you,' and that is?"

"You're choosing not to date me."

"You're choosing not to sleep with me."

"All you do is compare."

"All you do is play the victim."

"I'm not a victim! I'm an overcomer!"

"Overcome your bullshit past, then."

"Screw you!"

"I wish somebody would."

"I wish I had known my body was more important than my person! I would have never gotten married in the first place!"

Divorce

Writing memoirs infuriates me. How can someone go from surviving the projects to earning a doctorate, inspiring others publicly to conquer their demons, and obtaining all these accolades, but she can't piece together the pieces of her broken life? I guess the quote is true: "You can be at peace and in pieces at the same time." I couldn't stitch together the pieces of the tapestry. I accepted it whole, as it was, with beautifully interwoven threads of Egyptian cotton, bloodstains, golden rings, and burn marks.

I've overcome. I've infused others with hope and passion. I'm resilient. I've walked on. I'm the one who transforms vinegar to the teeth into champagne problems. I'm an inspiration, right? Right? David and I could do this, right?

We couldn't. Our divorce was stupid. Stupid in the sense that we said, "Until death do us part," and then our lives tore us apart. Stupid in the sense that one day we peacefully arbitrated our agreement, and the next, we fought over saltshakers. Stupid because when our hearts and bodies collided, we became one, but we couldn't hold, couldn't hold on through the pain and damage, and we left more pain and damage in our wake. Stupid because it hurt and tore and screamed and begged to be ended, but instead, we ended. We don't fight anymore, but we barely talk anymore.

Papa-Dad passed, and a piece of David passed away with him. We both ended up broken in our brokenness, and all I could do was see what I broke.

Self

I told my therapist I quit. She said I hadn't quit but made a choice.

I asked, "What choice?"

She said, "You chose you. That's not bad. You had a choice to make, and you chose you. You worked your ass off to save that marriage, but it couldn't be saved. You did your work, but you two couldn't love each other through your own brokenness, as you said."

"That's not selfish?"

"Selfish? I don't know. Self-kind? Yes."

I struggled with that statement for a long time. I still struggle. Does being a shepherd mean protecting my self-interest as part of the circle of life? I felt like the wolf. Or the witch. Or the dragon.

When I looked in the mirror, the little girl appeared. She had braided hair and missing teeth, and she smiled back at me. I saw a scar on her chest leading down to her heart. I looked at mine, and I had the same one too. I showed her my scar, and she showed me hers. I reached out to touch her, but I couldn't get past the reflection. We agreed we'd tell our stories from our side of the mirror and heal together.

Secret Keeper

Analyze

After reading this chapter, I feel

Shree Walker

Two Chairs

He ritually sets out two chairs every morning. Bob Beaudine, the author of *2 Chairs*, follows an intimate morning routine involving two chairs. Anywhere from two to eight feet apart, he sets these chairs, depending on how intimate the conversation. The older Bob gets, the closer he places the chairs: he's running out of time. At least here.

Bob meets daily with his Father. The routine is paramount and demonstrates his desperation to listen. The chairs don't matter; the presence does. Again, he's running out of time.

I am too. I've fought this battle for forty-five years now, and I hope to have forty-five more. Bob's created a good routine, and since I came from a family of dysfunction and anything but routine, I gave it a try.

I couldn't do it. Not the way I tried. I tried meeting with the little girl within, giving her space to speak, and I'd listen. I couldn't do it. I walked away.

Something didn't feel right. No, let me rephrase. Something felt *wrong.* When I pulled up the chair, the person looking back withered. Nothing in the mirror, only paned glass and a pained me. Where'd she go?

I stepped outside, inhaled, filling my lungs like overstretched balloons. I held my breath. *This won't work. Nothing transformational happens from pretending to talk to my younger self. It's just a mind game. I'm wasting my time.*

I'd been wasting time for years. I'd kicked the hell out of my boyfriend, tore through multiple relationships prior to that, and used my body as a washboard for somebody else's dirty laundry. Wasting time wasn't the problem.

Believe

I didn't believe her, and she didn't believe me. Well, she didn't believe in me. I'd hurt her too many times. When she made her list of abusers, I was number one. Every decision I'd made to hurt myself had hurt her. What did she expect from me? I'm not perfect. Hell, I'm her too. Only older, wiser, and more abused.

I didn't listen to her. She was immature. She had no experience, unable to look at these things rationally. Windswept by emotions, she'd never be free to heal. She couldn't. One in a constant state of hysteria can't heal, and she frantically banged around inside like an unhinged . . . child. That was exactly it. She was still a child.

We made a pair of untrustworthy, dysfunctional people. How could we heal each other?

Belief

I breathed deeply again. Anxiety set in. Panic even. Like a mother awaiting a diagnosis, my body fretted. Mutiny, again. *Stop it!* This mutiny screamed; I must have done something worthy for my body to fight against it so. I didn't abuse myself; instead, I tried healing myself. And the therapy hurt.

More deep breathing. Rhythmic. Slow. Calming. I could understand. I didn't need to understand everything for it to be true. I could understand how these two chairs—one stuck in the past and one in the present—worked.

One day, I saw a vision of a woman walking on the moon. I understood what I didn't understand. What I knew about life, laws, and possibilities,

I'd confined to my understanding of life on earth. Life grew lighter on the moon.

In this context, on this earth, I maintained a reasonable amount of understanding. Take me out of it, and I'd be clueless. My mind wondered, *What's possible on the moon?* I knew people changed when the gravitational pull decreased. Bodies grew longer; spines straightened; internal organs lost functionality; and vision decreased. In the meantime, I might run a two-minute mile on the moon.

"For every action, there is an equal and opposite reaction." That's what they taught us. Was that true on the moon? In space? If I lost torque running in low gravity, did I gain momentum by swinging my arms? If possibilities abounded in a context outside of earth, maybe possibilities abounded on earth that I didn't understand. Maybe some laws only exist in my mind.

On the other hand, some ideals transcend—like love. My grandfather died, and I still loved him. He was gone, but the love wasn't. One may argue that's one-way love. Fine. What about seemingly inexplicable connections? We sense when a loved one hurts miles away. We hurt. Identical twins separated at birth can live very identical lives. We sense danger unseen. We cry and laugh when someone long dead transmits an emotion through a written word. Or maybe just down the street. What about Ja? How did I sense something was wrong? Maybe communication exists outside of this life. Maybe I can talk to my younger self. She is part of me. I can at least listen.

Believe Me?

The abused cry, "Do you believe me?" in their hearts first before they cry with their mouths. An abused child has lost trust, so before they confide, they must trust. They cry in their hearts for trust, for courage, for protection—*before* confession. In the perception of their tiny minds, racked by terror and cynicism, revealing vulnerability would be foolish. Like believing a person could fly, move from point A to point B weightlessly, or run a two-minute mile. It's impossible, on earth.

Sitting in front of the mirror expecting eight-year-old Re to confess to me—someone she had no business trusting—demonstrated foolishness, a childish expectation on my own part. My own, grown self behaved more foolishly than a child. The conversation required cunning. I peered into my experience bag, searching for an other-worldly environment to cultivate the setting where she would be free to heal. I found nothing.

Believe me.

Extraterrestrial

I had picked the wrong setting. In my frustration, I charged outside to experience nature, hoping to find some solace. I found myself breathing deeply, inhaling the toxic fumes of the city, hearing the blare of car horns, and sensing the frenetic hearts of the drivers. I could have joined a glass-breaking party and found the same solace. I closed my eyes and wondered again, seeing myself in my mind's eye sitting on a park bench surrounded by bustling squirrels and rustling trees. That seemed logical; it always worked for me. As an adult. But I wanted to hear from a child.

I took the day to find myself, so I packed a lunch and headed for the playground. Children shrieked and laughed, played on the merry-go-round, (of course properly protected with all the modern-day safety equipment) and swung on the swings. As I watched them run and yell, recklessly abandoned to their specific moment of fun, it hit me—right upside the head. *Whack!* That's it! Play tetherball, lady!

Searching for a place to play tetherball in the twenty-first century is like searching for a pager. Only special people find them. I'm special. When I found the unmanned tetherball pole in a park—with the aid of Google—I delighted in my discovery. Then I frowned. Playing tetherball by myself seemed pointless. But my younger self remembered that all I had to do was strike the ball in one direction, and then hit it back the other when it came around. I'd done this hundreds of times.

My tetherball skills stunk. I whiffed the first strike. I missed the first return serve. I realized I'd be in for a battle. Not with an opponent, but with my old self. Slowly, I found the rhythm again, like riding a bike, and I enjoyed the activity. But nothing happened. Nothing other than working up a good sweat and catching some stares. Like I was crazy.

I know this sounds bat-crap-crazy, but I exploded. What the hell was I doing at this park, a grown woman, smacking around this ball like some séance? My inner child wouldn't speak to me because I knocked a ball around a pole like the earth orbits the sun.

I cried. I walked to my car, closed the door—and if I didn't look crazy enough—cranked the music and hit the steering wheel. I looked up at the sun, cried out, and discovered my mistake. Yes, as a child, I loved to play tetherball, and yes, I loved being outside. But I didn't appreciate it. That came with experience.

As a child, I appreciated the moon. That object fascinated me before many experiences did. I found something extraterrestrial again.

Extra Trust Required

Revolt! Seeking to set an appointment with my inner self had required too much time and energy. I create content, write, speak, meet, exercise, shop, listen, read, travel, and run a business. I didn't have time to placate myself with experimentation in "healing my inner child" or whatever psychological jargon I wanted to throw at it. I'd already wasted the day foolishly hitting a tetherball around a pole to an unseen opponent who clearly got the better of me.

Again, my body revolted. Thankfully, I recognized the mutiny. The unseen opponent wanted victory in my mind, not just on the tetherball court. Doubt wanted to block me from healing. Mr. Pain told me I looked foolish and that everyone would think me crazy. Why did they show up? Because a healed Shree meant a dangerous Shree. One who sought to help others rather than bask in her own self-pity. I'd be meeting with myself. Trust me.

Trust required more than I wanted to bring to the table, and I'd already learned the little girl within wouldn't show up without trust. I fought a duplicitous battle: one with myself to trust my instincts, one with my former self to trust my present self. No wonder people experience multiple personalities.

I knew enough about changing environments that creating a safe one was tantamount to feeding the lions before training them. But I didn't know enough about being a child anymore to know what to do. I sat in my apartment, staring at the ceiling, looking out the window, practicing being present, when I experienced a profound question, "Whom did I trust as a child?"

As an adult, I burned from experiences and flamed with mistrust, but as a child, things were not so. Surely, I didn't trust my father or my almost-stepfather, but I trusted someone. Teachers.

I loved my childhood teachers. I trusted them. I stopped trusting some workers in the education field at age sixteen—primarily those in administrative positions hiding impotently behind titles—but I loved teachers as a child, especially as a small one. And I still do. Some did bad things, as we all do, but the majority did good things. Good things day in and day out. At least on the job.

I made a plan and an appointment with myself. Then I created an environment. If little girl Shree needed an environment and a person she could trust, she'd have it. She'd already been through enough.

Extraneous

Overhauling environments entirely solves many issues in the classroom. I developed this skill during my second year of teaching. Likewise, doing it quickly and building ladders in the air came during my second year. Here was my plan: I'd build the environment, and I'd invite my younger self in.

In one day, I changed my spare bedroom from being a clean, spiritless room to a spirit-infused planetarium. I blacked it out with curtains, hung glow-in-the-dark stars and planets, and covered the walls. Marking off the Big Dipper proved challenging, but I wanted to "go in," so I decided to go all out. As much as a day's worth of work allowed on a shoestring budget. Shoestring because I didn't want to spend thousands on a one-day decorating experiment—and because some of the planets hung from shoestrings. Converse shoestrings, of course.

When I finished, I hung a huge, reflective representation of the moon, and I brought in the two chairs. One weighed more than the other; it held the weight of a little girl who'd been voiceless for quite some time. The chair came unwillingly, but I made it stick. I placed the mirror on the chair and turned the lights off. Back in my bedroom, I put on my most teacheresque outfit, complete with earrings and heels, and returned to my seat. The seemingly extraneous details mattered. Maybe the most.

Shree Walker

Like a conference, I pulled myself close to the mirror and spoke directly: "Now, Shree, you need to sit up here and look at me so we can discuss this assignment. I have high expectations of you, and I know you can do it. Let's make a plan so you can be successful." Not much of an invitation, but kids love formality and a challenge.

I stared at a reflectionless chair, fighting off the doubt, hoping she'd show.

Secret Keeper

Evaluate

Before reading this chapter, I thought

After reading this chapter, I now think

Shree Walker

Two Scares

The vision from the dark side of the glass appeared entirely in my mind. Unless possibilities on this earth corresponded with possibilities outside this earth. Unless angels and flying saucers, monsters, and aliens came from one unified source, we don't understand. Unless we rebelled against what we once knew to be true . . . she appeared!

Pigtails peeked around the corner, followed by a frightened face hiding a missing-toothed smile and bright eyes. She took the chair, straightened her blue and white dress, and crossed her legs, ladylike. I don't remember who taught her that, but she practiced it. She placed her hands in her lap and looked at me properly. Something burned underneath.

The next move was important. If delivered abruptly or passively, the entire interview would fall like shooting stars. I handed her the playdough. She pulled it through the mirror reluctantly. White playdough stains a blue dress. I held her gaze, and she looked away. *Oh no! I'm losing her.* Then I remembered she existed in me, in my mind, and she'd never leave.

She took the playdough in her hand, and I instructed her like I always instruct my students, "It is important now that you understand the *what*, not the *why*. The *why* will come when you learn to do the *what*. Open the playdough container, remove the playdough, and make something you'd see in the night sky."

I could have said, "And make a celestial being," but time would have been wasted on explaining nonsense vocabulary I could explain after the lesson. *I've still got it!*

She rolled the playdough into a perfect sphere, then plucked its edges into spires that she twisted into helix shapes. The once ball-shaped dough looked like a cross between Sonic the Hedgehog and Medusa: intricate yet gnarly. I remembered that painting. I couldn't recall the name, but I knew the painting from which she pulled the memory to form the starlet.

She spoke no words; her silence spoke for her. The childhood Shree chatted continuously once comfortable, but until that time, she had clammed up. My own starfish emerged . . . again. *Why am I sweaty? I'm the grown-up.* She waited. I got a clue. I rolled the playdough in my sweaty hands, peeling the paste from my palms, and made my otherworldly being. I left it as a perfect sphere, held it in my palm, and said two words: "Moon. Go!"

Her Turn

"Why didn't you help me? Why didn't you figure something out? Run away? Take me with you? Why didn't you tell someone sooner? Escape? Help me? I didn't want to go to the bathroom. You could have cried. Told him no. Yelled, kicked, screamed, told Momma, anything, but you stayed. You did nasty things. You obeyed. And you cried. What good did that do? You showed him we'd do it again. You didn't fight for me! I needed help, someone to take me away, and you did nothing! You pretended to fight. You kicked and screamed and yelled at all the wrong people. But you never helped me. Then you left me and gave in!"

She quieted. Tears welled in my eyes, stained my cheeks. Anger burned in hers. I hoped to see a spark of that old smile, but I got a deadpan face with hurt eyes.

"I've watched you ever since. You've done those nasty things over and over and over again, never giving me another thought. You brought me with you into those bedrooms, into those hotel rooms, never asking if it hurt me. I obeyed. I followed you and let you hurt me again and again. Even when you didn't want to do it, even when you tried to stop, you never talked to me. I had to watch."

I got pissed. I didn't choose all those things. Some were thrust upon me. Who was she to tell me of my evils and my failures? No child talked to me that way; I wouldn't have it.

She continued. "I didn't always obey. I got you back. When you married David, I got you back. You thought you could get married and make us a family, but you didn't ask me. When you tried to do those nasty things with him, I made you feel what I've felt all along. Afraid. Weak. Dying on the inside. Remember the time in the bathroom, screaming into the towel? That was me. Remember pacifying me with ice cream, then feeling sick to your stomach when he touched you? That was me. Remember the abortion?"

If I didn't believe in demonic spirits before, I felt like one spoke then. She didn't weep or frown or throw the playdough. She spoke. Straight-faced and chalk-eyed. I withered.

"Remember telling Momma? Telling your friends? Writing that book? Telling everybody but me that it'd be okay? You didn't tell them everything. You're afraid to tell them everything. You're afraid to tell me."

I made a mistake and spoke. "Afraid of what?"

"Afraid to admit you liked feeling special."

"Little girl, let me tell you something! I already admitted that. But *that* doesn't mean I liked *it*! I hated it. I liked feeling special because nobody made me feel special, and I wanted to be special. But let me tell you, I hated it with every fiber in—"

"Liar! You didn't hate it! You hated me! That's why you don't talk to me! That's why you left me! You're ashamed of me! You grew up and explained it all away, but you never said you're not ashamed of me. You only said you're not ashamed of you anymore."

Two Scares

She confronted me with my two scares: admitting I still blamed myself and admitting I still hated that little girl.

I'd grown proud of the woman I'd become: the strong, resilient, don't-take-no-crap-from-nobody woman. Yet I still hated the weak, defenseless, voiceless little girl.

I had a decision to make, and suddenly, I had a new scare. I didn't know what to tell her.

Shree Walker

Create

After reading this chapter, I will restore myself by

Two Scars

I showed her. I yanked the breast of my dress open, revealing the scar over my heart. A bold move, traumatic for the both of us, I'm sure, as I revealed my scar and feared not her response. I'd withered for too long, and I'd confronted the demons of my past. Even if the demon lived within me, was me, hated me. Listening no longer worked: I showed her!

"I am you! Look at your chest! I've carried you with me everywhere I've gone, and I've done all this to protect you. You're right, you were weak, but I made you stronger. You were scared, but I made you fierce. You were—"

"You made you stronger."

"Don't interrupt me—"

"I won't be quiet anymore. You made you stronger. I never asked for that."

"You didn't know what you needed. You didn't know what to ask for."

"Love."

I hung my head. "I'm sorry."

"No, you're not. If you were sorry, you would change. You would love me. You hate me. You only love yourself."

"How can you say that? I do love you."

"Then tell me."

"I just did. I said, 'I love you.'"

"No, tell me. Look at my dirty mouth and dirty knees and tell me you love me."

"I can't."

"That's why I hate you."

"You never showed me your scar."

"Why would I?"

"I don't say, 'I love you' to people I don't trust. You know that. I showed you my scar, but you never showed me yours. How can I love you if I can't trust you?"

"You're an adult."

"With the same broken little girl living inside me."

"Say it first. Because I can't love someone who doesn't trust me."

I paused. I believed momentarily in the possibilities, and I changed.

"Love doesn't require trust. Love loves even after trust is broken."

"You just said, 'I don't say I love you to people I don't trust.'"

"I was wrong."

"Again."

Tough Love

Love bears all things, believes all things, and hopes all things. Love never fails.

"I love you. I love you for the person you are. I love you for all the pain you've suffered, the hurts you've had, the fear you know. I love you even when you're weak. Especially when you're weak. I love you, and it doesn't matter what you've thought and said and did. I love you, and I'm carrying you out of here. I'm not leaving you locked in this one-way prison any longer. You can't live this way. We can't live like this. Stuck behind some wall only to watch and never experience because of all the shame. That's shameful. We're breaking out of here— together!"

She jumped through the mirror and landed in my lap. She pulled down the neckline of her dress, so I saw her scar, and she said, "I'm still afraid."

We moved the mirror, and she took her rightful seat. I said, "Let me love you through it."

Tough love doesn't always kick the other person's ass; sometimes, it kicks my ass.

My Turn

"This is going to be tough. You're not ready for all this, and you will not understand, but if you do what I say, you'll understand when the time is right. Right now, we're at the training ground. By the way, how'd you get so tough?"

She finally smiled that tooth-missing grin wide, and her eyes danced with excitement. "I learned from watching you."

"Take the playdough in your hand. Stuff it back in the container. Now take my playdough and stuff it in there too. Smash it in. Make it fit."

"It doesn't fit."

"Make it."

"I can't make it. I gotta take some out."

"Right. You can't make it all fit."

"Okay."

"Somebody taught you to make it fit, to keep it all inside."

"We gotta keep secrets to protect our family. We don't talk about some things."

"Right. But we must talk about some things. Look at the playdough. What happens when you smash it in there and press the lid?"

"Some of it oozes out."

"Right. No matter how hard you try, some oozes out. Usually on somebody else. Like David. You must be careful to take some out. Don't let it come out willy-nilly. Know what I mean?"

"Not really."

"Be selective. Choose what needs to come out. Do you hate your stepdad?"

"Yes."

"Is that helping or hurting you?"

"It keeps him from hurting me. I watch for him."

"Does it stop him? Is it helping you?"

"Sometimes it hurts."

"How?"

"It keeps me from having fun because I'm always worried he's going to come get me. And I want to love him, but he's bad."

"Right. And *he* you cannot control. But *you*, you can."

"Yeah, but what's my problem? Why did he touch me?"

"I have no idea. That's his problem, but you don't have a problem. You have a perpetrator—maybe a *villain* is a better word. He's the problem. You're not. How do you know what playdough to take out?"

"I don't."

"Let me help you. The playdough that's good and squishy, keep that. Use it every day. The dried-out playdough, the part that hates your stepdad and is jealous of your little sister, you've got to get rid of that."

"I don't know how."

"Okay, this part will be weird. Remember when I said you wouldn't understand right now? Here we go. You must admit it. You must look at it and say, 'Yep, that's me.' You don't need to like it; you just need to accept it. You have hate and jealousy. Then you need to talk about it with someone you trust."

She rolled her eyes, repositioning herself in the chair. "What if I don't trust anyone?"

"Talk to God."

"What if I don't trust him?"

"Stay mad. Be miserable. Hate everybody."

She whimpered. "Just because I don't trust God? That's not fair."

"Because you don't trust anybody. Listen, talk to somebody. Start with your stuffed animals. I don't care, but talk to someone you trust. Not just anybody! Someone you trust. The trust will come. When we hurt, we must deal with it."

"Do I have to talk?"

"For you, yes. I can't say for everybody, but for Shree Walker, yes, you gotta talk. Now listen, quit distracting me. This is important."

She batted her little eyelashes at me.

"If you try to protect everyone by keeping secrets, just like the playdough canister, you'll overflow. You must talk about the painful stuff. Tell on the person who hurt you. Tell on yourself. Tell your mom about your stepdad. Tell your dad you love him, even if he doesn't say it back. Take away the power of the bad stuff."

"What happens if someone hurts me because I talked?"

"They're already hurting you. Look at me. Almost forty years later. How many times have I been hurt because I didn't tell?"

"On them or yourself?"

"Both."

"Too many."

Two Steps

"Okay, I must teach quickly. We're running out of time."

"Why?"

"Because we have lives to live."

"You do."

"We do. Now you know step one: you gotta tell on yourself and others."

"Wait! Snitches get stitches. Snitches get stiches!"

"Look at our scars. So do victims. Steps two and three are to look in the mirror and to learn to dance."

She looked in the mirror and started twirling.

"Not like that! It's not two steps in one. First, you learn to look in the mirror, and next, you learn to dance."

"I thought you said step two and three, not first and—"

"You always were a smart . . . butt."

She smiled again. I loved that part too.

"Look in the mirror. Take a mental picture. Look in the mirror and look in your eyes. Tell them the truth. Speak the truth to yourself. Your eyes will show your lies."

"Okay, but my older self is crazy!"

"Good! That's the easy part."

"What's the hard part?"

"Remembering. That's why you do this every day."

"Why?"

"Not *why* but *what*. What to do every day is look in the mirror and remember. Remember who you are. Foolish people walk away and forget. Wise people remember."

"Huh?"

"Remember Leon?"

"Yeah."

"I forgot who I was. I let him project his needs on me. I became the crazy camping lady to keep him. Guess what?"

"What?"

"It didn't work. I lost myself in the process, and we hurt each other. A wise man once said, 'What does it profit someone to gain the whole world and lose himself?' In my case, what does it profit Shree to gain the whole world and lose Shree? Answer the question."

"What question?"

"What does a person gain if they gain everything and lose themselves?"

"All the candy and toys and friends they could ever want."

"And they can't look in the mirror because they hate the person they see."

"I'd like me if I had everything."

"I have cars, money, and men. Do you like who you've become?"

"Not all of you."

"Not the parts when I lost myself, right?"

"Right."

"Look in the mirror and remember who you are."

"Shree?"

"Do you still have his number in your phone?"

"Ouch."

"You should lose it."

"Moving on, step three is to learn to dance."

"I'm ready exhausted."

"Already exhausted."

I turned on some Cuban music. The beat hit. I tapped my foot and called, "One, two, cha, cha, cha. Three, four, cha, cha, cha." I stood. I did it again. I showed her the steps in place. "One, two, cha, cha, cha." She followed. She moved forward. "Back to your place! Learn the cha, cha, cha in place. One, two, cha, cha, cha! Three, four, cha, cha, cha!"

"One, two, forward, cha, cha, cha. Three, four, backward, cha, cha, cha!" I grabbed her hand and placed my other hand on her hip. We danced around the room, laughing and singing until the next song ended, and I pushed her into her chair.

"Ow!"

"Got your attention?"

"Yes!"

"Good. Learning comes in steps. You will not conquer everything in one day. It won't fit. You learn step by step. Move by move. Don't try to get it all at once. You'll miss the good stuff."

"But that's boring."

"When you learn to like boys, take it step by step. Start by liking, not seeking. Be a friend, not a secret. Then love yourself enough to respect yourself. Remember who you are. If you can't, walk away. If he doesn't, walk away. Everything comes step by step. Learn the steps before you try mastering the art. And, Shree, enjoy the steps."

"What if I forget? You said that I need to remember."

"It's okay. Remove things you don't need. Make room for the things you do. At eighty, I probably won't need to remember how to ride a bike anymore. But I will need to respect myself. That, I can't forget, and you can't either. Do you remember the two steps?"

"Yes, one, two, cha, cha, cha."

"No, silly. The two you just learned."

"Remember who you are and learn to dance."

"Close. Look in the mirror and learn to dance. What about the first step?"

"Let me think. I'm sorry. I don't remember."

"Remember the playdough?"

"It doesn't all fit?"

"What doesn't?"

"The stuff. Um . . . talk about it? Tell somebody and tell on yourself?"

"You've got it!"

"That's easy for you to say. You're big. You can go when you want. You don't have to run away to get away."

"Run away, then."

I grabbed her dress and held her in place.

"Let me go! Let me go!"

"You already forgot. There's always somebody bigger and stronger who can hold you back. That's why you tell. You can run away together. What if you told Grandma, or Auntie Bailey, or Dad?"

"They could help me?"

"Step by step."

"Okay, I'm bored now."

"Show me your scar."

"Why?"

"Show me your scar."

We both showed our scars.

"What can we do about these?"

"I guess nothing." She yawned.

"Can we heal them?"

"No," she said, yawning again. "I'm tired."

"Got it. We keep the scars, but we heal the wound. This should wake you up."

"What?"

"I've got something for you."

Secret Keeper

Apply

Because of my experience reading this chapter, now I will

Presentation

"**Hold out your hand.**" I placed a green, gift-wrapped box tied with a purple bow in her hand. "Open it."

"You got me a gift?"

"Open it."

She tore the paper open and pulled the gift from the box. She set the large, metal letter *B* on the floor and looked at me sideways.

"What's wrong?"

"Our name is Shree, not Bambi."

"Thank God. Can you imagine what that would've been like? Destined for the stage."

"Huh?"

"Sorry. You're right. What did I give you?"

"A *B*?"

"As in a . . ."

"Boy?"

"Another name for a gift is . . ."

"A present."

"I gave you . . ."

"A stupid *B* as a present."

"A *B* present."

"Can I take a nap?"
"Sure. Do you want me to leave?"
"No. I want you here."
"Present?"
"Yes." She looked at me sideways again, her eyelids drooping.
"Step to the window with me. If you want me to stay with you, I need you following me."

We looked out the window together. "What do you see?"
"Buildings, lights. That's about it in the dark."
"What about in the sky?"
"Only the moon."
"Right. Now what do you smell?"
"Sweat."
"What do you taste?"
"My dry mouth."
"What do you hear?"
"Cars. Horns. The cha-cha song in my head."
"What do you feel?"
"Tired."
"What can you touch?"
"I feel your dress. I feel the windowsill. I feel the warm air getting in."
"Good. A *be present* moment. A moment when you learn to be still. A moment when you don't chase loose thoughts or empty hurts. You learn to be present in the moment. If you want to be protected and be happy, then you must be present."

"Can I nap now?"
"Yes."

She lay on the floor and fell asleep in a second. Her silent snoring soothed me while I stared at the moon and let the exhaustion come wave by wave. The two chairs, the tetherball, the chasing, the anger, the decorating, the changing, the listening, the crying, the anger again, the feeling, the coaching, the sleeping . . .

When we awoke, slivers of sunlight seeped around the black-out curtains failing to do their job. Time wore thin, and the new day dawned. I only needed to teach her two more things.

"Shree, wake up, Princess."

I cried a lonely tear in that moment because my Daddy called me Princess. Shree rubbed the sleep from her eyes and rolled back over. I shook her, "Shree, wake up, Princess. There's not much time. Soon, you'll have to go."

She awoke. "Can I watch cartoons?"

"Yes. When we're done. Almost done. Sit with me." She sat in my lap, and I hugged her close.

"Before you fell asleep, we talked about being present. I'm showing you another way now. It's called meditation. Focus on one thing. Focus for as long as you can."

"I can't. I just woke up. I can't focus."

"Focus on the moon. Picture it like a big, white tetherball coming at you, and you want to whack it into oblivion."

"I can't."

"You can. Step by step. Here it comes. Don't hit it. Just focus."

"Good. You lasted twenty seconds. Try again."

"Good, thirty seconds that time. You'll get better step by step. Do this in the morning. Do this when you're stressed or angry. Do this before doing something important. Do this before you fall asleep."

"I am asleep."

"Last thing. Hold out your hand."

"Another present?"

"No. A pen and a pad."

"I know you're a teacher and all, but—"

"Write it down."

"What?"

"What you've learned. Write the numbers and write what you've learned."

"I hate writing."

"Step by step."

"Step one: tell somebody. Step two: look in the mirror. Step three: learn to dance. Step four: be present. Step five: meditate."

"How did you remember all of those?"

"I slept."

"Right. Sometimes what confuses us one day makes sense the next. Step by step."

"Learn to dance."
"You forgot one."
"No, I didn't."
"What did you just do?"
"What you told me to."
"Like?"
"Like make the list."

"Right. Write it down. It's called journaling. You can write your thoughts, emotions, things you've learned, what happened, what you did, anything you want."

"I hate writing."

"Then draw it, sketch it, label it, whatever, but put it on the paper. You'll remember better that way."

"I don't need to write it down. I'll—"

"How do you spell *Mississippi*?"

"I don't remember."

"Write it down. I have to go. You gonna do all the things I taught you?"

"You gonna ask me before you date your next man?"

"I hope so."

"I hope so too."

"Little girl, I love you. I've gotta go, but if you forget everything, just hold on to one thing, and you'll learn what you need to know."

"What? You love me?"

"No. Number seven."

"What's number seven?"

"Look at the moon."

Shree Walker

Understand

My experience reading this chapter was

Reflection

A good teacher leaves. A good teacher leaves the pupils wanting more. I've grown tired of moon metaphors, but one more begs me. Not bugs. Begs. Begs me to leave one more on the page.

Pupils contract in the light of the sun; it's too bright. Pupils dilate in the dark when the moon's out. I know about the sun and the moon and the light and the reflection, but the moon teaches me one more lesson.

I had left little girl Shree alone in the room until our next meeting. I pulled out the two chairs, and she climbed in hers. For me, it had only been a day. For her, time had passed. Years went by until she figured it out.

"I got it."
"What?"
"The moon thingy."
"Tell me."
"Shine your light."
"Huh?"
"Shine your light. When I look at the moon, I know it came from somewhere. It lights the earth with the reflected light of the sun. Shine your light."

"I don't follow." I did, but I'm a teacher, so I play dumb. Like a parent when their kid swears that he doesn't drink at the parties where everybody drinks. Until he gets caught.

"Shine your light. Don't hide it."

"You got it! Good job!"

"You don't."

"What are you talking about?"

"Last year, when you gave that 'Words of Gratitude' speech at Freemont."

"Right."

"You prepared for weeks. You knew you'd say, 'If you're a Pathfinder, you're in good company. And if Dr. Shree Walker's not enough, you're in good company with Dr. Dre.' You skipped the drill down."

"Drill down? I know you're grown and all now, but what's the drill down?" She'd aged some since our last meeting—no longer a child.

"Only about 2 percent of people have a doctorate, fewer if you're female, fewer if you're Black, and fewer if raised in poverty. I did it, so anything is possible. And if that's too much for you . . ."

"Taco Bell sells wings!"

"Why'd you do it? I'm with you, but the little girl inside doesn't always know why the big one wants to hide."

"Have mercy, child! Now you have rhymes?"

"Why'd you dim your light?"

"Because I didn't want to upstage the next speaker."

"Then you did the right thing."

"No. I did the wrong thing. Sometimes we only get one shot to say or do something that changes a life. Sometimes ours. They asked me to do a job, and I didn't deliver my best."

"But what about when you're with friends, and it's their turn to shine?"

"You remember who you are and use your resources to help them shine. That day, they called me to speak."

"You spoke—then choked!"

"Like your jokes! I can rhyme too, remember?"

She looked bored again. Teenage Re was sassy, independent, and stubborn. Time to end this thing.

"You missed something."

"No. I wrote it down. Step one: tell. Step two: look. Step three: dance. Step 4: be present. Step five: meditate. Step six: journal. And step seven: shine your light!"

"Look at the moon."

"Huh?"

"When you don't know what to do, look at the moon."

"I thought you said that shining your light was right."

"It is."

"I'm confused."

"Clearly."

"I know I'm supposed to respect my elders, but you're working my nerves, and I only got one."

"Look at the moon. Believe in the possibilities. Look at the moon. It reflects the sun. Something is always greater than you. When you don't know what to do, look at the moon."

"And . . ."

"Maybe the One who's greater than you will show you the way."

Shree Walker

Analyze

After reading this chapter, I feel

Secret Keeper

Trippin'

Take the trip in. Dr. Robert S. McGee, in his profound book *The Search for Significance*, introduced an inspired method of self-investigation he aptly titled "The Trip In." I'm not qualified to reproduce the methodology here; however, the process requires exploring my reactions, rationale, and relationships before I respond. I am truly thankful for Dr. McGee's work, and I respect it highly.

I created an issue when taking a trip in to explore my reactions, rationale, and relationships by using my own method: I manufactured a trip up. Searching for information on my abuser resulted in a bad kick and a good story. I searched back through my relationships with my father, No Name, Lafayette, José, Marcos, Leon, and on and on, but I only evaluated what I could have done differently to control the situation. I ended up with empty lists. In the end, David and I paid the price. My trips in destined me for a trip back to a past I could not change and a story I could not untell.

I also wore the wrong glasses. I mined through my past with a magnifying glass searching for clues like Sherlock Holmes, not Superman. Holmes sleuthed for someone to blame; Superman flew for someone to save. *Why have you made me thus?* Versus, *Why have you saved me thus?*

Shree Walker

Dad

Dad and I drowned in the same ocean, wandered in the same wilderness, clung to the same cliff. I came from him, but we disconnected early and fought alongside each other in a war of mutual separation. Craters formed when we collided, and unbridgeable canyons alienated us though we called across the distance, "I still love you. I just don't know how to show you."

My relationship with my father was tenuous at best and downright cataclysmic at worst. We colored together and cussed each other out. He bought me dresses but didn't watch me twirl. I kept my own secrets but couldn't love him for his. We floated in and out of each other's lives like ghosts trying to embrace.

We didn't stick. If someone asked me, I'd tell them, "I've made every attempt to reconcile with my father." If someone asked him, I'm sure he'd say he made every effort to provide for and reconcile with me. We knew how to give but not to receive.

Today, we talk and we accept. I see him more frequently now that I've moved back to L.A. Hopefully, our time together continues to increase. We'll see.

Shree

The conversation with my younger self in the previous chapter was a good "trip in" for me. I told myself what I needed to hear, listened to my own needs, and came away with my own advice. Advice I needed to take. The little girl within spoke, heard, and was heard. She got a voice. I got a lesson.

I still believe I must investigate my past as well as myself, but with the proper perspective. Not to wallow, but to heal. Not to blame, but to help. Not to scrutinize, but to save.

The little girl within wanted to love, not to hate. She provoked change based on love, not fear. Change because I want strength, not because I fear weakness. If I change for fear, I'll always run from my past. If I embrace my past, I'll run into danger, saving others, saving myself.

I almost titled this book *Choosing Me*. I stuck with *Secret Keeper* because I'm the secret, and I'll keep myself. I won't lose myself. Lose my life, yes. Lose myself, no.

I've exposed my past, dealt with my past, forgiven my past, and now, I'm moving forward, leaving my past behind.

Like I do.

I gave myself to this book, and now it's time to receive.

God

As I wrote, trusting my dad created frustration. For the longest time, I didn't. I didn't accept him. As a result, I projected those same feelings toward my heavenly Father. I didn't trust. I did it my way. I chose me.

I came from God, but we disconnected. Now we're reconnecting. I used to believe in forgiving others and forgiving yourself. But I believe differently today. I believe I can change, and I can be forgiven. I can change and choose to forgive others. I can receive forgiveness from God and others. I grew in giving forgiveness but not in receiving. Then I learned I must receive it also. How can I give myself something that's not mine to give? Now I try to receive and accept God on His terms.

He accepted me with all my brokenness, rebellion, and secrets. I can accept that. By choosing Him, I choose me, the me I want to be, the Shree I want to see.

Dying to myself, losing my life in the process, but not losing myself. God is good at giving and receiving. If I give myself to Him, then He will receive me, and I will be Chosen, Noticed, Known, Special, and most importantly, Loved.

This Here I Must Say

When I finish a presentation, I use an activity titled "This Here I Must Say." I pull the framework from Bloom's taxonomy—a guide for expressing the levels of learning—and I address the disruption caused by the presentation. Throughout my book, I dropped breadcrumbs, focusing on the *what* and not the *why*—so what must you say now? Below are the statements:

1. Understand: This experience was
2. Analyze: The truth is I now feel
3. Evaluate: I used to think . . . but now I think
4. Create: I will restore myself by
5. Apply: Because of this experience, I will

Now let's focus on the *why* behind the *what*. The *why* is peace and disruption do not have a contingent relationship . . . but they can live in harmony.

Secret Keeper

Evaluate

Before reading this chapter, I thought

After reading this chapter, I now think

Shree Walker

Peace

I need peace. I seek peace. Peace doesn't fall in my lap like breadcrumbs from a grilled cheese sandwich; peace is a state of being. It's how I "be." It's how I am. And like a range of emotions—disgruntled, fearful, exuberant, and joyous—peace comes and goes. But in the tumult of life, peace must be sought. It's worth finding. It's worth sticking around for.

Picture a still pond: the descending sun casts amber and violet rays on the clouds and shimmers of light upon the water. Trees guard the pond, shaken ever so slightly by the breeze. A lily pad or two float listlessly near the dock where you recline, drinking your most relaxing drink. *Ah!* Peace.

Picture what occurs beneath the water. A violent struggle ensues between a fish and a turtle. A large bass snacks on a small minnow. A frog tangled in the moss takes his final breath. A water moccasin traps a crayfish, and all the while, you rest peacefully on the dock, with the breeze on your face, feet reclined, content.

In the midst of the chaos that you don't see, you have peace.

Now picture a raging forest fire. As the forest creatures escape to safety, you realize the inferno encircled you. The only way out is through. Within the fire, death certainly looms. Where's the peace?

Within you. Peace exists within you.

On the pond, the circumstances are peaceful. Under the pond, the creatures war. In your heart, by the pond, or in the fire, you may contemplate death or life. A man considers suicide by the pond as easily as in the fire. A woman considers suicide on the beach as easily as in the desert. What about in the delivery room? Can a woman be at peace when the life within her struggles against her life without?

Peace exists inside, despite the circumstances outside. And peace must be sought.

Disruption

When I mine through my past, it creates disruption. As one can tell. Digging through it to write this book caused disruption, major disruption. I got disrupted. My boyfriend got disrupted. I erupted.

Disruption comes in all forms and fashions and usually reveals something underneath—where no peace exists. I've seen a woman get disrupted over her blackened fish at Red Lobster being black. She ate the whole thing. I've seen another erupt at Starbucks because they didn't have a cake pop. Really? A cake pop? I've seen a man have a meltdown over cheese and an entire family over the last doughnut. Have you ever seen a person dying of cancer live in peace as a family member died next to them over a thread in their jeans? I promise it's not about the jeans.

Disruption occurs underneath, inside, in the hidden parts of the multilayered being. Disrupted, too, is a state of being, not a circumstance. Peace and disruption are states of being. They are not, however, independent or interdependent. They just *are*. Which means they coexist.

Remember the soda bottle? Inside, the locked and loaded soda teems with carbonation: carbon dioxide disrupts the liquid (water) within. Under pressure, the soda bottle explodes due to too many external conditions. The water bottle, on the other hand, contains peaceful water. As long as no other substance gets inside, the water remains pure. Too much heat may boil the water and burn the plastic, but the water douses the fire beneath. Too much cold may freeze water, but the water transforms back to its original state when it melts. It's at peace. Only something getting in the water contaminates it. The water remains at peace with all sorts of disruption occurring around it. (Yes, the water can transform into steam and evaporate, but don't ruin a good science analogy with more science. That's disruptive.)

Let's just admit it. We all have a little carbon dioxide floating in our water, so we must seek peace (more water) to dilute the impact of carbon dioxide. And for me, seeking peace means making room for disruption, so it can exist while I maintain peace.

Making Space

I make space. This *here* I must say. Making space for disruption is imperative. Enter books and Bloom's. I could substitute books with another circumstance, but for this analogy, I'll stick with books. I wrote this book. You are reading this book. Both processes caused disruption.

We typically read books for one of four reasons. Or all four. In my explanation, I will use knowledge and experience synonymously. We read books to gain knowledge, enhance experience, reframe knowledge, and affirm experiences. The experience disrupts our thinking. I've cried, laughed, choked, kicked, screamed, and trembled while reading a book. Some I've had autographed, and others I've thrown in the trash. Reading books disrupts. Writing books disrupts. Experience and knowledge both disrupt, so we must make space.

Hello, Bloom's taxonomy! When I present, I know the presentation creates disruption, so I end the presentation with the five statements from Bloom's. That way, we make space for and understand how we feel and what we believe about our experience. The goal is *not* to create disruption; the goal is to seek peace *during* and after the disruption. I'd love for you to respond for yourself.

1. Understanding. What was your experience? What must you say after this experience? Finish this statement: "This here I must say . . ."
2. *Analysis*. How do you feel? Do you feel grateful, remorseful, bold, exuberant, slow, or satisfied? Maybe you don't know how you feel. Then give me a quote or a thought that encapsulates a takeaway from the experience. Complete this statement: "The truth is I feel . . ."

3. *Evaluation.* What did you think before, and what do you think after? Did you used to think spilling the beans was stupid, but now you think keeping the beans inside creates eruption? How has your thinking changed? Finish this statement: "I used to think . . . but now I think . . ."
4. *Create.* To restore yourself, what will you do? Will you go for a run, see a therapist, visit the park, or make a salon appointment to restore yourself? Or will you have a drink, shoot some pool, play a video game, eat some popcorn, or do the cha-cha to restore yourself? (Admit it: you want to do the cha-cha too.) Finish this statement: "To restore myself, I will . . ."
5. *Application.* Because of this experience, what will you do? Will you make amends for your wrongs, so you can live with no regrets? What will you do? Finish this statement, "Because of this experience I will . . ."

This is what I call a Mindset Meter, I use the Mindset Meter to know what I am making space for and from. It tells me how desperately I need to recharge and why.

Carencia

One time I met a man. No, this isn't another one of *those* stories. He had a tattoo on his forearm. Shepherd? Maybe. Angel with scars? Possibly. Man with a tattoo of some word I didn't know on his arm? Definitely. The word, *carencia*, was Spanish. He explained the meaning to me, but the significance evaded me. Why tattoo a word that connotes "a shortcoming" on his body? I didn't understand. I stopped to analyze. Like I do.

I felt confused by the tattoo but intrigued by the man. Maybe his explanation missed something. I continued to evaluate Something felt *off*. I investigated and learned that *carencia* represents a break that a bull takes from a matador during a bullfight. That made sense. A bull makes space; frustration requires we do the same. But I did not understand the significance.

I searched. I watched videos, read articles, and looked at pictures of bulls. They're not beautiful creatures, but they do possess the appearance of quiet strength. Although they might look intimidating, their mass and horns failed to impress me. But their eyes did not. Their eyes said, "There's more going on inside me than you know, and if you push too hard, you'll see my resolve." Quiet. Strength.

I finally found it. I read an article by Ruth Ann Rose on the meaning of *carencia*.[4] The bull retreats to *carencia* when he gathers his strength. His momentary pause allows him to regroup, to quiet his rage and frustration, to calm his fears. He knows he's weak, so he's frustrated. He knows he's strong: he's a bull. At that moment, he's meekness embodied—strength under control. And there he builds.

Carencia means "a lack." But not for the bull. For when the bull appears lacking, he's rebuilding. He's making space for his fight. He's preparing, peacefully. The battle lies before him, and even if he surrenders, the prodding will come. He waits, strengthens, and resolves. He resolves to attack with vigor, but only in his *carencia* can he do so. Without it, he's a weak male cow who can't control his temper. He's impotent.

And then he attacks. Although he may lose the battle, he fights with control. He no longer sees red. He sees relief in the fight, not the victory. He's at peace.

Healing hurts. The process of healing unearths wounds and issues that tug on our very souls. The process surrounds us with unfavorable circumstances: emotional pain, pressure, instability, constraint, and it reminds us of our weaknesses.

Did anything you read do that for you? Did you feel weak, bitter, resentful, angry, scared, scarred, judgmental, overwhelmed, frustrated, shamed, or hurt by the experience? If so, how will you heal? How will you make space? Where do you truly measure on the Mindset Meter really? Don't lie to yourself; it won't make you special. Just crowded. And carbonated. Understand, analyze, evaluate your mindset—then act.

I make space by following the seven steps I outlined for the little girl Shree. I make internal space because I can't control all of the externals, such as when I don't get a cake pop at Starbucks or my brother takes the

---

[4] Ruth Ann Rose, "Your Power Is in Seeing Your Lack," Medium, June 14, 2018, https://medium.com/@ruthrose321/your-power-is-in-seeing-your-lack-44d56f8a2eba.

last doughnut, and I have to eat burnt fish instead. But I can control the internal, to an extent. And what I can't control, I turn over to God. Because chaos can't control him. He is Peace

Shree Walker

Create

After reading this chapter, I will restore myself by

.

Create

I cannot create a tadpole. That's beyond my realm of expertise. But I can create an opportunity. And I can make a difference. I can't change my DNA, but I can change my perspective. And I can create an opportunity to change my perspective.

I am not the same person at the end of this book that I was at the beginning. I'm forty-five, give or take a few years, and I'll be different at fifty-five, sixty-five, and so on. Because of my experiences. Because of my circumstances. Because of the disruption. And I can be at peace, seek peace, and bring peace.

I can be a Mr. Jensen.
A Mr. Jensen?
Yes, a Mr. Jensen.

Be a Mr. Jensen

A sensational video resides on YouTube as a tributary commentary of an action a teacher named Mr. Jensen took.[5] His student, Clint Culver, retells the story of being unable to sit still in class. He tapped. A lot. He moved

---

[5] "Be a Mr. Jensen," May 4, 2017, YouTube video, 3:12, https://www.youtube.com/watch?v=4p5286T_kn0

and wiggled and tapped his fingers and pencils on the desk. The students yelled, "Clint, stop tapping!" He couldn't. The teachers yelled, "Clint, stop tapping!" He didn't. The principal said, "Clint, sit on your hands!" He tried and failed. Mr. Jensen also yelled, "Clint, stay after class." So Clint did.

Mr. Jensen peered into Clint's eyes as Clint sat across from him. Clint shuddered. He knew trouble had found him again. Mr. Jensen asked one question. "Have you ever thought about being a drummer?" Then he reached into his desk and handed Clint a pair of drumsticks.

Clint, a ten-year-old boy with an obvious deficiency, took the drumsticks and threw them in Mr. Jensen's face, and stormed out of the classroom. His deficiency defined him. He had no peace. *Carencia* failed. He couldn't sit still.

Maybe that could've happened, and Mr. Jensen's day would have turned into a nightmare. Or he could put the sticks back in the desk for another day. But that's not what happened or what matters. What matters is what's on the inside. And inside Clint, a drummer grew.

Clint took those sticks and played the drums. He eventually paid his way through college playing the drums, and he began touring the US and the world playing the drums. Otherwise, a video wouldn't be on YouTube. Clint found his *carencia* playing the drums. The peace existed in the disruption, in the deficiency. And the disruption ceased.

Mr. Jensen found his *carencia* too. He created it. Not the *carencia*, but the opportunity for it. Clint could have tried and failed, but it's significant that he tried. That Mr. Jensen tried. That Mr. Jensen sought peace. Made an opportunity for it . . . which brings us back to Bloom's.

Because of this experience I will build empathy for others, create opportunities for the less fortunate, call my dad, seek to help the abused, guard my mind and body, or whatever I decide. Whatever you decide. What will you do because of this experience? Your mindset matters. Will you seek peace? Will you create the opportunity for peace within yourself?

I like how the twelfth step of Alcoholics Anonymous articulates this action: "Having had a spiritual awakening as the result of these steps, we tried to carry this message to alcoholics, and to practice these principles in all our affairs."⁶ The twelfth step can be used by anybody; just substitute "alcoholics" with your preferred group. Here's the point: Writing this book and saying, "Oh, that's good," is not enough. I do good by practicing and sharing. You do too. I'll go first.

I will restore myself from this disruption for disruption because I'm not keeping these secrets anymore!

Although disruption and peace live as states of being, they can be causal. Sometimes, peace brings disruption, and sometimes disruption brings peace.

Peace, be still.

---

⁶ *Alcoholics Anonymous: The Story of How Many Thousands of Men and Women Have Recovered from Alcoholism*, 4th ed. (New York City, NY: Alcoholics Anonymous World Services, 2001), 60.

Shree Walker

Apply

Because of my experience reading this chapter, now I will

Secret Keeper

Shree Walker

Secret Keeper

Acknowledgments

I thank G. K. Chesterton for writing: "The baby has known the dragon intimately ever since he had an imagination. What the fairy tale provides for him is a [hero] to kill the dragon."[7]

I thank my younger self:
For believing in the possibilities.
For holding on to those possibilities.
For believing being fully alive is possible.
For enduring the challenges of life.

I thank God:
For protecting me while I operated in the flesh, not the Spirit.
For making me his daughter.
For providing the affliction I needed . . . because I needed it.
For teaching me I don't belong in the wilderness.

I apologize to those I hurt directly and indirectly:
For being a villain in your story.
For bringing you into my affliction.
For making you part of my story.
I hope you can offer some grace.

---

[7] G.K. Chesterton. "The Red Angel." In *Tremendous Trifles.* London: Methuen & Co., 1909. 170.

Shree Walker

I thank my readers:
For understanding even villains have stories.
For believing the true person comes from the flame.
For seeing good in me.

I thank Michael Ison:
For being a secret keeper until the time for publishing.
For helping me share my story.
For remembering I am human.

I thank Jared Austin:
For challenging us to communicate clearly and authentically.
For fleshing out the details.
For protecting me.
For understanding truth is truth, no matter how raw or real.

I thank the men with whom I've had a relationship:
For helping me learn to live out loud.
For showing me to live while I am living.
For teaching me addiction to being unloved is wrong.
For proving I am way too fly to be somebody's number two.
For loving me in a way that caused me to become myself.

"No man is your friend, no man is your enemy, every man is your teacher." ~ attributed to Florence Scovel Shinn

www.ingramcontent.com/pod-product-compliance
Lightning Source LLC
Chambersburg PA
CBHW030435010526
44118CB00011B/641